The Self-Correcting Organization is available directly from:

NorthWest Training And Development
111 Ridgecrest Road
Thunder Bay, Ontario, Canada P7B 7A1
(807) 622-6077   www.nwtd.ca
Or at www.selfcorrecting.ca

Quantity discounts are available to organizations,
educational institutions and associations for
re-selling, educational purposes, employee
presentations, conferences, customer promotions,
subscription incentives or fund-raisers.
See "Self-Correcting Resources" on page 139.

Tellwell Talent
www.tellwell.ca

ISBN
978-0-2288-1593-8 (Paperback)
978-0-2288-1594-5 (eBook)

THE
SELF CORRECTING
ORGANIZATION

Building Reliable Performance
and Recovering from Error

GARY PHILLIPS

Dedication

This book is dedicated to YOU. Yes, you. It was written for one purpose only - to offer insights and techniques for your use.
You honor me when you select relevant learnings
and apply them in your organization.
So from me to you, I thank you most humbly and
wish you great success – make a difference!

Gary Phillips

TABLE OF CONTENTS

INTRODUCTION

Thanks for being curious enough to read this far. I take it as a solemn duty to deliver on your expectations.

This book was born from a long simmering frustration about outdated assumptions and clumsy practices in organizations. Practices that I've seen within otherwise tremendous management systems. My professional career has involved years of training leaders and hearing their frontline stories and frustrations, and of consulting in a wide variety of organizations.

Experience reveals patterns.

One pattern sees supervisors and managers sent for training without their leaders inquiring about either the content or their own role in supporting the subsequent application of learnings – over-training and under-implementing. Another shows frequent consensus about issues amongst people closest to the front line whose input is then undervalued or ignored. Yet another involves shallow use of systems and resources without disciplined attention to context, to potential ripple effects within complex systems and to human factors.

Consulting and training share similar frustrations with parenting adult children. When adult children have problems, make mistakes, or exhibit poor decision-making a parental dilemma rears its head. A parent no longer has authority over these adults yet they're deeply committed to seeing them succeed. How do we influence respectfully without damaging relationships and while increasing the other party's available options and personal resources?

Although the patterns that this book reveals, to build reliable performance and recover from error, may seem obvious, they will challenge some of your conventional wisdom. Yet I'd be surprised if the insights awaiting here don't, at the very least, ring bells, provide an "Aha!", or leave you feeling "That should have been obvious all along."

When a parent or an outside resource person who is without direct authority finds ways to influence respectfully, that's success.

So too, when you nudge your organization towards self-correcting performance from within you role-model what self-correcting systems are all about! Waiting for others to initiate or until you garner more authority yourself will only generate more frustration.

Perhaps our own paths may even cross one day. I look forward to the possibility.

In the meantime be disciplined – apply your learnings, build new connections, see new patterns. And pay those forward. Lifelong learning for both us and our organizations ensures self-correcting systems will outlive us for generations to come.

FORWARD

The Secret of Life

James Taylor put it succinctly, as he often has, in his song "The Secret of Life", describing it as "enjoying the passage of time." Not too shabby an insight.

A shorter version is:

Keep moving!

Move in as many ways as possible, that are meaningful to you. Move to preserve the health and safety of yourself, and the people and the environment around you.

Or to paraphrase Albert Einsteiin. - Life is like riding a bicycle. You need to keep moving to maintain balance.

OK, I thought I'd get away with "keep moving" but, as the Chairman of the Board said, "That's Life!" Just when you think you've got a handle on it, it always gets more complicated.

Through decades of personal and professional development experiences in consulting and training and through exposure to the work of folks smarter than myself, I've noticed another "secret." It's one that underpins this volume, applies well beyond its covers, and cuts though the complexity.

So this book, initially about safety investigation, had an affair with other ideas and ran off in the middle of the night to seek "Fame and Fortune" (the two imposters). Then it morphed into a book about transforming organizations into self-correcting entities through existing mechanisms, building performance reliability and responding effectively to error. Yet on a personal level it still carries echoes of that embedded "secret", the one that enables us to enjoy life, whether at work or in the pursuit of life in general.

So here it is, Gary's version of the "Secret of Life" (a bonus for those of you who had lesser expectations).

> The "secret" of life is mastering the ability to maintain resourceful states, both consciously and unconsciously, to enable you to make good decisions on a minute-by-minute, second-by-second basis to optimize life experience for yourself and those around you.

From this flows everything else. Chew on that awhile.

Actually this book has no ambitions that you buy into some great "secret" or belief.

Rather it simply offers useful ways to think about performance reliability and errors in organizations and how to respond to them in practice. This includes tools and techniques for you to pick and choose from. Many will serve you well beyond the workplace.

From routine activities, to non-routine, to emergencies, we have to build and manage performance reliability in different ways. After a downgrading incident, from initial reaction through analysis and remedy, how we manage some form of investigative response, be it casual or formal, sets the tone for an organizational intervention that is critical to the development of high reliability systems.

As you read you'll find it useful to keep the following assumptions in mind:

- Context matters! The ways you manage your people during routine operations will probably not work during non-routine and emergency situations.

- Error events are normal human performance phenomena. The sooner you accept that, the sooner your organization will thrive.

- The most influential factor shaping your organizational culture is error tolerance.

- Applying blame and linear cause/effect thinking to human performance shuts down ongoing system-wide learning.

- Much of what you learned in the past about safety and particularly about investigation may no longer be relevant.

- By re-shaping the way you use existing systems for training design and incident investigation, you can transform your organization.

While you're enjoying this book, maintain your own resourceful states. And have fun! You learn better with a healthy sense of humor. Which reminds me of the one about the talking dog…

Gary Phillips

Thunder Bay, Ontario, Canada

ABOUT THIS BOOK

The Self-Correcting Organization

So what makes for a "Self-Correcting" organization?

In the same way that high functioning performers use mental models of what normal situations or performance must look like, so too organizations build proactive performance and learning systems which require a clarity of standards or references to "normal" performance. This is the starting point for reliability and the prevention of future error events.

In *Safety Management - The Challenge of Change* (Hale & Baram, 1998) the authors include a chapter by Mathilde Bourrier titled "Elements for Designing a Self-Correcting Organization: Examples form Nuclear Power Plants". After a caution regarding the dangers of investigator bias following error events, she references several points that describe the "normal functioning" of high-risk organizations:

- ...paradoxical as it may sound...in order to follow procedures, one has to be able to modify them on the way. As one mechanic...explained: *"We have a procedure. We are expected to follow it exactly. But it's easy to come to a point where it doesn't work. But we have to follow it...a failure to follow and you are in big trouble."*

- The rigidity of a highly proceduralized Safety Management System may even endanger the integrity of the organization and its members, mainly because adaptation is not quick enough.

- What are the underlying organizational factors that account for rule following as opposed to rule breaking? It depends on the work structure, the design of responsibilities and/or access to resources, whether the unavoidable modifications to procedures will take place, either openly and legally or secretly and illegally. The reason that such modifications do not always take place openly and legally is that only some organizations have built-in processes that enable workers to modify rules and procedures.

So the performer who identifies the need to adapt a procedure to get the job done, but who believes that if they do they'll be in "big trouble", will be unlikely to make such adjustments. If they do make the adjustment they will be unlikely to report it for fear of punishment. So organizational growth and learning stall, except for the informal sharing amongst peers of the "secret" tricks to make things work.

Alternately the performer may just call their supervisor every time there's a variance and take no initiative. Again organizational learning and adaptation stall. And hapless supervisors find they don't have enough hours in the day to do all the trouble shooting.

Interestingly in our Leadership training workshops, such supervisors are the ones who seem to be called out most often to answer calls from work. Most of these calls come in two categories – either people don't know what to do and they have competency problems in dealing with variances, or they need permission to do something and there are problems with distribution of authority. Often these supervisors present with overt expressions of stress and work/life balance issues. These, in turn, affect their ability to maintain resourceful states on a daily basis.

Bourrier goes on to say: "A successful self-correcting organization can thus be described as an organization capable of inventing explicit (as opposed to tacit) mechanisms to cope with unavoidable tensions between prescriptions and the reality of work situations."

She adds by quoting M. Landau (1973) *On the concept of a self-correcting organization*, Public Administration Review, 33(6) 53-539: "'Scientifically managed' systems cannot be scientific unless and until they are set on the foundations of criticism. For this is the only way to make an organization accountable, effective and reliable."

And even though organizations often perceive themselves as open and encouraging feedback, the reality in staff or safety meetings is that few will speak up (except amongst themselves at the break after the meeting). They feel it's not safe to speak. I spoke up last time and got shot down. I offered input but never heard back. I spoke up and my peers ridiculed or ostracized me afterwards.

So let's imagine an organization with built-in mechanisms that offer continuous improvement (Self-Correction) without any wrenching system changes! These mechanisms wouldn't demand new "programs of the year", but only that we continue to do what we've already been doing, albeit more thoughtfully and carefully.

But how?

In Part 1 we consider three proactive mechanisms that address the characteristics of Self-Correcting Organizations referenced above. Chapter One addresses how we move authority around as operational context changes and how training must adapt to accommodate each shift. Chapter Two provides a set of questions to analyze any performance management problem. And Chapter Three asks us to reconsider our training designs – particularly task analysis.

In Part 2 we examine a fourth opportunity, one actually required by law in many jurisdictions - Incident Investigation. Within Incident Investigation lies the golden opportunity to improve organizational function with the least amount of turmoil – by reshaping perceptions of blame. This fourth opportunity links back to the other three proactive, pre-incident activities that build reliable performance.

A *caution* regarding Part 2 - as we examine Investigation, particularly in response to human error in the workplace, we'll encounter troubling questions about past practices and assumptions. This section invites us to conduct Investigations quite differently than they have traditionally been done. I'll explain as we go, but first...

Cancer makes you better looking?

I had a cancer experience a number of years ago and learned a remarkable thing - cancer makes you better looking!

This may sound preposterous but it's fully evidence-based and to date there have been no exceptions. Here's how I know. Up until that cancer experience no one ever walked up and spontaneously told me how good looking I was. But afterwards, without exception, people have come up and remarked that I was looking really good. (They often omitted the "for a guy who should be dead" part.) This continues to the present day. Were we to meet in person it would probably be obvious to you as well.

If you're questioning my logic, you're not the first. Yet I regularly find logic like this in the workplace. Many "pundits" profess that their programs for transforming a workplace are highly successful and that their success is "evidence-based." Apparently this is because they installed a program and then something changed.

Now I'm a big fan of things that work. And I'm always delighted when a cause/effect relationship can be shown to explain something that's otherwise puzzling. But personally, the "pundits'" logic often escapes me.

The most reliable process to "prove" a cause/effect relationship in the physical world is the scientific method. We hold all variables constant except for the one that we control and change. Then we study the effect and determine if a relationship can be established.

But in my 30-plus years of consulting and training in the workplace, I don't see much rigorous scientific methodology "proving" that programs delivered anything more than a Hawthorne Effect (See Wikipedia – Hawthorne Effect). Instead I see situations involving multiple variables within dynamic changing workplaces where erroneous assumptions about cause and effect are regularly made. Such assumptions, particularly where human error is a factor, often lead, not to progress, but to blame and other unwanted effects on the operation.

As physicians know, the first responsibility is to "do no harm." Likewise, managers, human resource and safety professionals, external consultants, and really all of us within a system are responsible, at the very least, to not make things worse.

Yet many of our current models of "causation" and our assumptions about how things work can fall prey to this same "correlation/causation confusion." This is akin to my proving how much better looking I apparently am after the cancer experience. Things that are related to one another do not necessarily imply a causal relationship.

In fact, searching for "the cause" is a big part of the problem. It leads to the question "Why". And, as we'll learn in Part 2, asking "Why?" in relation to human action is problematic unto itself.

So I make no claim here that *The Self-Correcting Organization* is a scientifically researched program that will transform your world. In fact it is not a "program" at all. It does however draw from extensive practical experience. And it offers a carefully chosen collection of approaches that encourage a different way of thinking about building reliability and responding to error in the workplace (and beyond should you so choose). And it includes a set of techniques that have proven useful in reducing the risk of doing more harm and in promoting faster organizational recovery. As such these will bring transformation with them. Many are currently in use in high reliability organizations such as aviation and nuclear power generation.

Websites and workshops are dangerous?

When the precursor to this book, *The Art of Safety*, was published, one of the promotional strategies was to submit it to professional associations for consideration and review. The goal was to have the book included in their resource libraries or to become a choice at their bookstore.

Many of these associations were kind enough to review the book. One decided not to include it in their bookstore because the book made suggestions to go to a website for additional free resources and to consider workshop attendance to learn behavioral skills associated with the book's content. These were skills which could not be mastered without practice. Such suggestions were dubbed professionally inappropriate.

If you have similar concerns, you risk limiting your professional development. Many of the skills described herein are best mastered with practice and feedback. I encourage you to seek out related information, do your own research, talk to others and find learning events that allow for skills acquisition. You can find resources at the end of the book. At the very least grab a learning partner and practice.

Non-verbal communication expert Michael Grinder has often lamented the tendency to "over-train and under-implement." You can reverse that trend by finding appropriate learning opportunities that provide the skill practice and behavioral feedback required to master your new skills. When you consciously repeat them, they become automatic parts of your repertoire.

What to expect

Again The Self-Correcting Organization is *not a program*. It is a **way to think** about reliable performance, operational failures and errors, and your response to them.

And it offers a **series of techniques** from which you can pick and choose.

It *is* about:

- How different operational contexts require different management approaches
- How to easily diagnose performance management problems
- The power of effective Task Analysis
- Investigator mindset
- Personal skill enhancement
- Developing respectful influence
- Enhanced interview techniques
- Accountability and forgiveness
- Analysis through learning teams
- Recommendation Analysis

It is **not** about:

- Physical conditions and systems (i.e. engineering or ergonomic analysis)

Human unreliability and equipment risk cannot be managed in the same way. Equipment does not present itself with free will, competing interests, variable attention or intentionality, at least not yet.

<u>Application</u>

These approaches and techniques can be applied across the spectrum of workplace experience:

- Performance Management
- Training and Development
- Patient Safety
- Response to:
  - Errors
  - Failed Plans – Strategic or Operational
  - Injuries, incidents
  - Equipment damage
  - Environmental discharge
  - Violence/harassment/discrimination
  - Organizational failures
  - Problem solving
  - Audits

Many of the interview techniques are also immediately transferable to employment interviews and counseling applications.

<u>And why bother with the investigation piece?</u>

When things happen the eyes of the organization focus on that operational area, those people, that process. There's a rare pause in day-to-day operations that allow us to examine our systems and figure out how well they are working or not working. Investigations offer that pause. And, in many jurisdictions, investigations are required by law. Management and workers are expected to cooperate in analyzing and developing responses. What a unique opportunity!!

The expected outcomes, of course, are recommendations to prevent further downgrading incidents and improve operations. Performance reliability improvements are at the heart of such recommendations.

Try this thought out.

If prevention is the primary goal of investigation and you're still experiencing repeat incidents, it's likely your current investigations are not working the way you hoped.

Read that again.

When a mechanism intended to provide continuous improvement doesn't work, the effects ripple through every part of the system.

Consider this. Every question asked within the organization is a mini-intervention. If I ask someone, "What can we do to improve things around here?" I've already created an expectation in that person that something will happen as a result of their input. If nothing ever happens, or they never hear back, then the next time I ask how we should improve I'm more likely to get an "I don't care, whatever you want" response.

We directly shape people's experience of the organization by how well we handle ourselves interpersonally, particularly during investigations and inquiries. This will then shape their performance in "normal" performance situations and their response to variance when adaptability is required.

If an innocent question like "Why?" can take us where we least expect, then imagine where in-depth interventions, clumsily handled, might lead.

An organization's level of error tolerance will profoundly shape its culture.

Keep in mind that an organization's response to error and its level of error tolerance will directly shape its safety and organizational culture in profound ways.

Stop thinking about investigation as a chore!!!

It's *the* on-going mechanism to make your organization a self-correcting one.

And embrace the fact that performance happens in a variety of contexts that demand different approaches.

Any of us can literally be the change agents who transform an organization simply by adopting different approaches to tasks you're already doing.

Will it be easy?   **No.**

Will it happen overnight?   **Definitely not.**

But can it be the most satisfying experience of your career? Without doubt.

Having committed many of the classic mistakes and moved past them I can personally attest to this.

Pushing against other peoples' beliefs or their ways of doing things, often produces resistance. It took me a long time to accept and recognize that the resistance was a comment on me, not them. I told you this wouldn't be easy.

And having "test driven" the concepts you're about to master in workshops over many years we've received consistent feedback. That it's "about time", "a breath of fresh air" and it's "consistent with what we already know goes on".

Changing beliefs and installing new practices requires that we acknowledge and enter other peoples' versions of reality. It's the only way to build rapport. Once we've demonstrated our willingness to listen and understand their viewpoint, whether we agree with it or no, only then can we move out from that point into new territory. Only then will we begin to hear honest accounts of what really goes on at the front line. And nothing is more satisfying than successfully nudging people toward innovations that make a positive difference for them and the organization.

Remember you don't deal with another department or a layer of management or a stakeholder, you deal with a *person* in that department, at that level or who represents that stakeholder group.

So let's begin with the context(s) within which we work to build reliable performance. After all, "It depends" is not only an answer, it's a path to the appropriate question.

Then we'll examine the current state of performance and error response in many organizations. We'll ask where, despite our best intentions, have we strayed off the path? And how we can get back on course.

PART 1

BUILDING RELIABLE
PERFORMANCE

CHAPTER 1

IT DEPENDS – CONTEXT IS KING

My entry into organizational development and performance management came through occupational safety and workplace training. I had graduated from university and teachers college just as the leading edge of the Boomers already filled the available teaching positions in our area. So I spent 7 years as a municipal firefighter, then moved on to manage the health and safety function for the municipality.

What an opportunity it was! I was free to wander through an organization of some several thousand people from the CAO to the front line, in a wide variety of functional areas, and often when they went into error mode. I couldn't have bought a better organizational education. I should have been paying them!

Safety and training can open doors that reveal how an organization ticks. This is truly profound! It amazes me how little senior management taps into this insight.

And more recently I'm stunned by the number of organization leaders who send their good folks out to learn leadership or training skills but never ask for a briefing on the content of what their people are learning. How can they follow up and reinforce those learnings? Some seldom even inquire about what's on the minds of the people who are running their organization for them! What a way to cut themselves off from the very pulse of the organization!

Senior managers will not get information that others think the boss might not want to hear. Nor do they get feedback on their blind spots, the ones that are perceived to be too career-threatening to point out. This can be a serious issue for senior leadership. Am I getting a clear and reliable picture of what's actually going on? Or am I getting smoke blown at me?

Sometimes referred to as the "Jar Jar Binks Syndrome", after the much maligned character of the Star Wars prequels who prevailed past the first movie despite the howls of the fan base, or sometimes as the "Emperor's New Clothes", senior managers can be seduced into justifying actions that are contrary to the collective wisdom of the organization. Jerry Harvey's "Abilene Paradox"(1988) refers to this as collective trips to Abilene that nobody wants to take.

Safety and training functions, including patient safety in health care, are an untapped source of such collective wisdom. They are also ideal starting points to initiate organizational change through existing systems. This avoids lapsing into "flavor of the year" cultural change programs that are often poorly understood, poorly executed and viewed with distinct suspicion.

Later we'll focus on the management of the Training Design Cycle and the Incident Investigation process as logical points of entry for organizational interventions that build high reliability.

Again, this does not mean we can continue to manage and use those existing systems in the ways that they traditionally have been managed and used.

Back in the day as a young and diligent disciple of the safety movement, I learned and echoed all of the prevailing mantras of the day - pursue loss control, safety is job 1, all accidents are preventable, "0" is a laudable goal, search for unsafe acts and conditions, and so on.

My sincere and heartfelt apologies to any of you to whom I promoted such unexamined concepts. I hope this book will set the record straight.

One of the delusions of my developing career involved the assumption that once we had set standards and procedures and trained the performers, then it's a simple matter of managing compliance. This is basically a regulatory approach to performance management.

Of course it turned out that it's not one approach versus another, but again, an "it depends" answer. And more so than ever, in this day and age, it's useful to get comfortable with paradox and ambiguity.

Rather than looking for some "Holy Grail" of an intervention, think about the insights and skills you develop as a toolbox at your side. Your effectiveness comes when you can *assess* what's in front of you and select the right tool. A hammer won't work when you need a screwdriver. A screwdriver won't work when you need a wrench. And secondly you need to *master* each of the tools through application and practice.

After all of the Visions, Values, Missions and strategic plans have been set, performance management starts with the establishment of clear standards. No evading this whatsoever! Without clear standards of what a good job, well done is and what acceptable and unacceptable behaviours are, people can't be trained, held accountable, or managed. Yet we've always assumed that once standards are established, we're off to the races. After all, haven't the regulatory bodies given us passing grades for having standards and procedures in place?

But there's a snag. How do we know that our standards are reasonable? OK, they satisfy legal compliance and often go beyond - to err on the side of safety as they say (an irony worth exploring). But is that enough?

The snag is that standards and procedures often do not fit all of the contexts in which we operate.

Now we could create more standards, and then even more again, to cover any eventuality. And if every possibility could be foreseen, if we had the resources to spend all our time writing more and more standards and procedures, and if doing so would not muddy the already complicated waters of human performance, then great.

But everything cannot be foreseen, we don't have unlimited resources, and complexity in and of itself significantly impacts human performance.

Context is King

So *it depends*. And context is King.

Standards and performance only make sense in relation to the operating circumstances that prevail. Every shift in operating circumstances requires that standards be re-evaluated and adapted. Emergencies are different from normal operations. When our backs are against the wall financially, we operate differently. We take more risks. On weekends and evenings with fewer resources around, people get the job done in different, creative and often non-standard ways. If we punish them because they step up to solve a problem that existing standards don't fit and it doesn't work out, few will attempt to try such adaptations again. This is how culture gets shaped. Once again:

THE MOST SIGNIFICANT FACTOR SHAPING AN ORGANIZATIONAL CULTURE WILL BE THE PERCEIVED LEVEL OF ERROR TOLERANCE.

If honest attempts to deal with non-standard situations are viewed retrospectively as errors and then punished, then most adaptation, honest reporting, learning and creativity will evaporate. And as honest reporting diminishes the leader is left without insight into the current operational context. Essentially the leader can still be convinced that they should stick with a Jar Jar Binks character or that their new (non-existent) clothes really are admired by all.

<u>Basic Context</u>

Let's examine three basic categories of context - each of which requires different standards, authority distribution, procedures, training, and management:

Routine, Non-Routine and Emergency

Each of these needs to be handled differently, even though they're inexorably intertwined. Thus some approaches, tools and techniques will overlap as well as stand alone in their own context.

Routine, Non-routine and Emergency situations are the basic foundation levels of context differentiation. Of course there are many specific aspects of context, including timing, resource availability, market conditions, legal demands, weather, seasonality, life cycles of equipment and human resources. Shifts in these and innumerable other variables allow us to identify <u>when</u> we must shift from Routine (stable conditions) to Non-Routine (variable and uncertain) to Emergency (variable, uncertain, and an immediate threat of damage).

Let's examine them in turn.

Routine

Most of our systems and controls have been created to manage routine circumstances. Most of the time they serve us well.

The path to reliable performance during routine operations will come as no surprise. Resource libraries are filled with volumes of management and leadership texts that show us the way. It's not the goal of this volume to reproduce those. You already know the usual suspects – clear corporate values, vision, and mission; thoughtful strategy; well-defined standards, procedures, roles; responsibility and authority limits; appropriate goals; robust coordination and information movement between functions, levels and units; flexible management; self-correcting systems; and so on.

The variables we deal with during Routine operations are generally controllable. We have reliable information and we have sufficient time to apply standards and procedures to a given task. The requisite resources are available.

Our goal is compliance.

Our generic tools include procedures, control systems, checklists, and specific mental models (ways of thinking about things).

Training for Routine operations can be done in slow time using standard training techniques - Demonstrate - Practice - Correct. As well, regular supervisory coaching, mentoring and performance management techniques can be applied.

Non-Routine

So when do we exit Routine situations?

Changes in the level of complexity (the number of controllable or non-controllable variables), the quality and quantity of available information, and the available time are the principle indicators that context has shifted, that adaptation to Non-Routine is required.

This can happen from things as seemingly innocent as the difference between day and night shifts, the replacement of one veteran member of a team, holiday season, increased demand for productivity, or aging equipment.

In Non-Routine situations additional variables arise. Routine actions do not produce expected results. Information is limited, distorted or unavailable. We may or may not be in a time crunch. Required resources are either unavailable or insufficient.

The goal becomes increased vigilance, and adaptability to respond beyond the Routine.

Our standard tools - procedures, controls, checklists, and mental models may still be reapplied or they may even include trouble shooting options for Non-Routine circumstances. Some performers will repeatedly apply standard procedures without success because they don't recognize the need to shift into the new context.

If the time frame allows for consultation to a higher level of supervision or management, deference to authority can still be engaged. But the level of initiative and control taken by the frontline operator, worker or professional increases. As subject matter experts, the frontline person begins to take more control of the adaptive or problem-solving process. Management's level of control shifts automatically as they defer to expertise.

Training for *foreseeable* occurrences and the use of problem-solving techniques can be conducted as if in Routine situations. However, preparation for the *unexpected* Non-Routine event must be expanded to include Situational Awareness and Decision-Making, so that people can make discriminations about context changes, while maintaining themselves in resourceful performance states. Training for such events needs to include more scenario-based practice in response to Non-Routine situations rather than simple re-application of routine procedures.

Emergencies

Emergency situations present even greater complexity in terms of increasingly uncontrollable variables and less available or reliable information. But what sets Emergencies apart is the time frame – the need to act immediately to contain further damage or injury in order to save lives and/or stabilize operations.

This need for immediacy of response requires that the frontline person assume control. To take the reins of leadership. The time limitation no longer allows for deference to authority. Ad hoc consultation with other subject matter experts (SME's) may be engaged if time permits. Existing mental models may no longer fit. Thinking "outside the box" increases. The responder must exhibit a preference for decision-making and action when undo amounts of time for analysis are not an option. Think about the first aider who is taught to quickly assess, take charge, decide on a course action, and then act. (You direct traffic! You call 991! You get the first aid kit!)

The management structure has ceded control to the person at the point of the action. The locus of control shifts from authority to expertise. Examples of failures in rigid command and control structures that demanded strict deference to authority abound!

Accounts suggest that during WWII in the Pacific, the United States Navy lost fewer aircraft carriers than the Japanese. When a Japanese carrier was hit, the rigid command and control structure left sailors waiting for orders on how to proceed while

American sailors immediately organized themselves into ad hoc teams to jury-rig a patch so the carrier could limp back to port.

Preparing people for emergencies no longer looks like traditional training. Real world simulations with full sensory involvement, an element of surprise (We'll have a fire drill this month but I'm not saying when) and robust de-briefing are required. Then practice, practice, practice. Consider the pilot who goes though annual simulator training that offers full sensory emergency scenarios in real time.

Once again training for emergencies requires inclusion of Situational Awareness techniques, mental models geared to adaptive problem solving, and ways to maintain oneself in a resourceful state under pressure.

The following figure illustrates how control by management versus by expertise trades places as we move from Routine to Non-Routine to Emergencies. It also summarizes the key points for each of the three contexts.

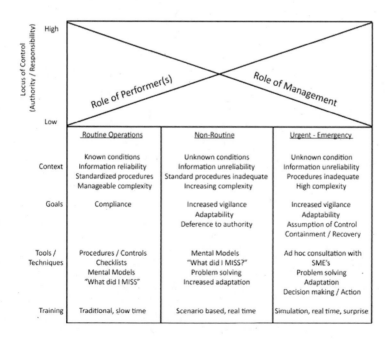

	Routine Operations	Non-Routine	Urgent - Emergency
Context	Known conditions Information reliability Standardized procedures Manageable complexity	Unknown conditions Information unreliability Standard procedures inadequate Increasing complexity	Unknown condition Information unreliability Procedures inadequate High complexity
Goals	Compliance	Increased vigilance Adaptability Deference to authority	Increased vigilance Adaptability Assumption of Control Containment / Recovery
Tools / Techniques	Procedures / Controls Checklists Mental Models "What did I MISS"	Mental Models "What did I MISS?" Problem solving Increased adaptation	Ad hoc consultation with SME's Problem solving Adaptation Decision making / Action
Training	Traditional, slow time	Scenario based, real time	Simulation, real time, surprise

As our Training Designs and our Investigations produce recommendations that impact training, standards, facility design and performance management, we must ensure that they cover and are adapted to all of the operating circumstances (Contexts) in which they will be applied.

Of special note is the development of, and impact on Standards. As mentioned earlier, without clear standards for a good job, well done, and for what acceptable and unacceptable behaviours are, people can't be trained, held accountable, or managed.

Do you have clear standards not just for Routine situations but also for the foreseeable, Non-Routine and for Emergencies? Do performers have the requisite authority to make adaptations for circumstances where normal procedures don't work? If they took the initiative and it didn't work would they be praised for taking the initiative or punished for making an error?

In Chapter 2 we'll examine a universal performance management tool, a set of questions for diagnosing performance problems and putting them into perspective.

CHAPTER 2

WHAT'S THE ISSUE?

Over three decades, we've fine-tuned our Leadership Development workshop series based on one thing – feedback from the participants. We listened to what worked in the real world and what did not. The only content that remained was what works in reality.

One tool that withstood that test of time and of practical application is "What's the Issue?" It's Gary Phillips' set of six questions that allows you to diagnosis the bulk of performance management issues and point to the type of intervention needed to address those issues. See *The Art of Safety* (Phillips, 2008).

<u>What's the Issue?</u>

1. What's the **standard**?
   - What's a good job, well done? In terms of Safety? Quantity? Quality? Timeliness? Completeness?
   - What's acceptable versus unacceptable behavior?
2. Is the standard **reasonable**? Is it clear?
3. Who's **responsible** to carry out the standard? Is that clear?
4. **Can they do it**?
   - Is it a **competence** issue?
   - Do they have the skills and knowledge?
   - Is it an abilities issue?

5. **Do they do it?**
   - Is it a **compliance** issue? What's the frequency of non- compliance?
   - Do you have reliable evidence?
6. Are the necessary **resources** available?
   - Time? Materials? Equipment? Authority? Budget? Info?

1. What's the Standard? What's a good job, well done?

Standards are the basic building blocks of all performance management. Without a clear standard of what constitutes a good job well done, we can't manage. If we haven't specified the standard, we can't admonish someone for "not doing it right." We can't train. We can't even inspect.

Include acceptable time frames in your standards. Many workplaces have lots of procedures, but not enough standards, including a time frame. For example, to replace a pump, a procedure exists covering lockouts, tags, removal, replacement, and testing. But the fact that an hour and a half is a good job, while three hours is not, is not included. So the performer who accomplishes the task in an hour and a half gets "rewarded" with more work, while the person who takes longer gets put on an easier task. As the "go to" person realizes they're not getting paid any more than the person who doesn't have to do it, they can easily drift into complacency themselves.

We often get more of the behavior we reward.

A frequent question is "How detailed do I have to be with standards anyway? Shouldn't they know what to do, or how well to do it, without being told to the nth degree?"

Specific

General

Imagine a vertical scale, from "General" standards at the bottom, all the way up to "Specific" at the top. If I ask someone to clean the room and I offer a general standard, it sounds like this, "Do a good job, see you later." At that point, whatever I get depends on the interpretation by the performer of what a "good" job is and I have to live with that. At the other end of the scale, I might say, very specifically "Grab the mop with your right hand, but not the left. Move your left foot first but not your right and start in that corner, not this one. And go up and down, but not side to side." Come on do I really have to go into that much detail?

Go into as much detail as needed until you could draw a line across the scale and say, "Beyond this, any other interpretation that the performer makes of a good job, well done, I'll live with."

Now your inner voice may be saying, "I shouldn't have to do that", but if you're not getting what you want, it's exactly what's needed. The best gift a leader can give the performer is to be crystal clear on the desired standards. Just don't expect they'll always agree with you and say thanks.

For instance, we all have different beliefs about what the speed limit on the highway should be, based on our own driving experience. Maybe, for some excellent drivers, it could be raised and they could still drive safely. For other drivers maybe it should be lowered. However, law enforcement can't manage by saying, "Well, just drive whatever speed you think is safe." A standard must be set so we can manage, despite individual opinions to the contrary.

Our interpretation of the job will often differ from that of the person who carries it out.

REMEMBER: As a leader, if you're not getting what you want, you reserve the right to say more about what a good job, well done is.

You may hear, "They don't have to do this in the other departments" or "…on the other shift". One response is, "You don't work in the other department or on the other shift. We've got processes for responding to concerns about inconsistencies. In the meantime, this is how we do it."

– What's acceptable versus unacceptable behavior?

Amazingly, standards for some of the most important things often are not in our job descriptions, procedures, or agreements. Consider the example of the phenomenon of "transparency." (Phillips, 2008) It begs a standard that says, "When we make a decision, based on our agreed upon processes, we expect you to support it as if it was your own, and not passively or actively sabotage it by publicly blaming others in the hierarchy and fostering a lack of respect." Although this may be one of the most important standards for all organizations, we're often hard pressed to find it recorded or even articulated anywhere. The standard can't be enforced if it doesn't exist.

We get the people we deserve.

In one client organization, departmental performance issues were ascribed to a "lack of respect." The implicit expectation was "be respectful." Now that's a general standard if I've ever heard one! This led to a tense, conflict-loaded environment. So standards were clarified, not only for job tasks, but for interpersonal behaviors, along the lines of: "Don't walk away when someone is talking to you." "When you're finished your work and someone else is not finished hers – go help her, without being told." "Don't talk about other people behind their back."

You shouldn't have to tell people some of that. But if you're not getting what you want, be crystal clear up front on what behaviors are acceptable and unacceptable. That's what leaders get paid for! Making up standards "on the fly" only makes people feel like they've being singled out.

2. Is the Standard Reasonable?

Is the standard **reasonable**? Is it clear? Is it consistent with legislative and industry standards? How do we determine any variations?

The big challenge is that reasonableness changes, maybe even from second to second. If I'm a physician under normal operating conditions, I'll try to save everyone if possible. But if I'm doing triage after a major disaster, I may determine that this person will die anyway and leave them, that one will live anyway and leave them, and then focus on the others who can be saved. This would be unthinkable in normal circumstances but is perfectly reasonable during a disaster response.

Every time operating circumstances change, the standards need to be re-examined for reasonableness.

Workers do this regularly without thinking - night shift versus day, financial crunches, weekends versus weekdays, shorthanded, and of course Routine versus Non-Routine versus Emergencies.

Context Matters

Performers regularly adapt standards anyway to get the work done during changing contexts. If they take the initiative to solve a problem, it doesn't work, and they get chewed out for taking the initiative, they will be less likely to take a risk in the future.

The most important thing a supervisor or manager can do with their crew or department is to huddle regularly to discuss whether the standards for a good job well done are clear enough and if they're still reasonable given the current operating circumstances (context).

Read that again.

3. Who's responsible?

Who's **responsible** to carry out the standard? Is that clear?

You'd think that our organization charts, job descriptions, and supervision would make clear who does what. And in most cases they do. But echoes of "That's not my job..." or "Someone should clean that up..." or "It's everyone's job to keep it clean..." can still be heard.

Assigning responsibility is required for clarity. It must be done face to face, and visually, regarding all aspects of performance. "I need *you* to clean this up so that..."

4. Can they do it?

Can they do it? Do they have the skills and knowledge?

If the Standards are reasonable and clear, and Responsibilities are clearly assigned and you're still not getting what you want? Ask, "Can they do it?"

Do a Competency Test. Can they explain what needs to be known about the task (Knowledge)? Can they demonstrate what has to be done (Skills)?

Keep competency records.

Too many organizations keep *training records* that involve an attendance sheet and a sheet for the learner to sign that they "think they understand." The latter is simply an opinion survey. What if they didn't get it? What if they're deluded?

Stop keeping training records. Oh yes, have them sign-in but **keep competency records**. Ensure that learners demonstrate the knowledge and skills in front of the supervisor or trainer. Then have that supervisor or trainer sign that they, the supervisor or trainer, witnessed that demonstration of competence. That's what satisfies your due diligence!

If people don't have the skills or knowledge, the prevailing remedy is training. Make sure your training is well designed, user-friendly, sufficiently long enough, and delivered by people who themselves have the skills and knowledge needed to assist the learning. And be ready to acknowledge that getting all that right can be more challenging than saying, "Hey, show the next person what to do."

How often do you train? If your training is well designed, well delivered, and followed up on to ensure implementation, then it probably needs to be delivered only once. Human beings are learning machines, without peer.

Of course, individual learners will vary in the length of time they need to learn and, possibly, in the way in which the learning is made available. If a performer still cannot perform the task to standard, even when the training satisfies our criteria for flexible training, then the *ability* of that performer, in relation to that task, bears examination.

Is it an abilities issue? If yes, training probably won't fix it. The options are transfer or termination.

Periodic refresher training for important competencies that are not used regularly, or that are legally mandated for a regular repeat, are a different matter. Ensuring a demonstration of competence, rather than repeating the entire training over again, is the best strategy. The frequency of such refresher training is determined by the *complexity* of the task and the *importance* to the job. For example, CPR (Cardio Pulmonary Resuscitation) training is often refreshed more frequently than general First Aid because of the *complexities* of mastering the required timing and compressions. And a first responder might practice with the mannequins even more frequently because of the *importance* of that skill to the job.

5. Do they do it?

Do they do it? Is it a **compliance** issue? What's the frequency of non-compliance? Do you have reliable evidence?

Now, if you've clarified the Standards, and Responsibilities, and witnessed demonstrations of Competence, and still aren't getting what you want, ask, "Do they do it?" Is it a Compliance issue? Can they do it, but don't?

Make sure you have reliable evidence. Keep records. Don't rely on hearsay, but don't ignore consistent hearsay either. Confirm compliance by being present more frequently to observe the performance yourself. (This can be tricky with professionals operating independently, self-regulated professions like doctors or lawyers.)

Would it be useful to consider why this behavior may be occurring, especially if it is not the "normal" behavior? Would it be appropriate to gain insights into why they aren't doing it? For example, could a person with personal issues benefit from access to an Employee Assistance Program?

**Occasional events of non-compliance are
the responsibility of the performer.**

**Repeat non-compliance, three or more times,
is a supervision or leadership issue.**

While this is plain, it is not always simple. If there are repeated incidents of non- compliance, take a good look at the management system – intervention begins with the leader, not the performer.

6.   Are the Resources available?

Are the necessary resources available? Time? Materials? Equipment? Authority? Budget? Info?

Organizations find themselves in varying states of access to resources, depending on the usual variety of business and environment issues.

What happens when we *don't* have the resources to get the work done and satisfy the standards?

We have to go back to the top and change the standards, often to a chorus of objections to a new expectation that people do more with less.

Keep in mind that the elements of a Self-Correcting Organization discussed in the Introduction and Chapter One on Context require that Authority be redistributed as context changes to ensure that standards are reasonable for each context.

And beyond that?

What if we reach the limit? What if we can't ask for, or get any more from, our equipment, or our people?

Then, back you go back to the Mission. What is our primary business? Can we still be in this business with the available resources and meet the standards? Can we complete the Mission operating as we are doing now? Do we need to contract out? Are we still consistent with our Values and Vision?

Ask the six questions to determine where to intervene when things are not happening as they should. Use them as a checklist as part of your due diligence.

"What's the Issue" can be applied throughout the organization at any level.

You may find yourself applying the six questions at one level and then need to re-apply them to the next level above as well.

As you apply the questions to certain levels and functions keep in mind that one often overlooked area is interdepartmental or inter-level coordination, planning and supervision.

Here's an example of applying "What's the Issue?"

When I started with the municipality, the Standard for staffing on a garbage truck was four workers – two slinging cans and bags, one driving and one in charge. As funding became tight (Resources) and they saw that other municipalities were successfully lowering the size of their collection teams (Reasonable) they went to three people. Still later, as funding got tighter and more municipalities started lowering the numbers again, they went to two people on a truck. Of course such changes do not generate a lot of "Gee thanks" reactions but ultimately the organization moved on and the garbage collection still got done without undue numbers of injuries as a result.

One step beyond that example are those cases where private services have taken on garbage collection with one person both driving and loading while offering the same level of service, making a profit and often cheaper than the municipal service could have delivered it.

When we cannot deliver performance to meet our standards and have no more resources to draw from, re-examination of our mission is paramount. What businesses can we be in? Often at this point contracting out is considered.

Sequence

Keep in mind that "What's the Issue?" is presented in a sequence. We cannot hold someone accountable if we haven't ensured that they were first competent and aware of their responsibilities. We cannot design or deliver training for competence unless we have clear standards of performance and behaviour that are reasonable for the operating circumstances that the performer will be put into.

Our leadership workshop participants are expected to memorize the "What's the Issue?" questions by their second training session. They even get a wallet card of the questions as a learning aid. Consider that strategy. Make a copy of the questions and keep it handy or in front of you until it becomes second nature to ask the questions each time you assign work to performers.

Even as you continue to develop subtle communication and respectful influence skills (many of which appear in Part 2), keep in mind that as skillful as you may be interpersonally, unless you take care of the basic "What's the issue?" questions first, they will come back to haunt you.

CHAPTER 3

TRAINING DESIGN

When we run Train the Trainer workshops, we include a segment on Training Project Planning. We suggest the following scenario to the participants: Imagine your boss comes to you one day and says, "We've got a new process (or piece of equipment or procedure or regulation) coming in. Make sure everyone is trained up by the end of the year."

This scenario allows us to explore the big picture of training design and to challenge the trainers to identify how much of that design cycle they are responsible for. Not surprisingly their boss often has no idea of the implications that such a directive implies.

So before we hone in on Task Analysis, here's what the Training Design Cycle looks like.

Training Design Cycle

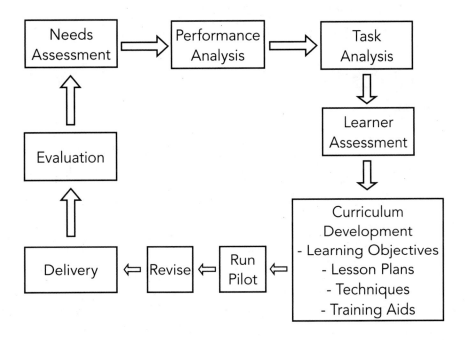

Needs Assessment

Training design begins with a <u>Needs Assessment</u>. Proactively it considers what's coming that requires a training intervention – a new process, new equipment, new regulation, workforce demographics, competition, or mandated refreshers. Reactively it considers performance issues, injuries, damage, failed plans, requested skill development, and so on. At the end of the needs assessment, a list of potential training needs has been generated and prioritized.

Performance Analysis

Needs Assessment is followed by <u>Performance Analysis</u>. How do you know it's a training problem? Ignoring this step can lead to inappropriate training interventions that are unnecessary, costly and counterproductive. It was certainly where I made many rookie mistakes as a Safety Professional.

One of the dirty little secrets for safety people is that operations and maintenance generally don't want to see you coming. So when they say they actually want some safety training, we're like happy puppies. Somebody finally needs us! An overeager response can miss the question "How do you know it's a training problem?"

I was once asked to address hearing conservation issues through training – what's the risk, where's the exposures, and how do I protect myself – the usual content. So we dutifully designed and delivered multiple sessions, spent lots of the organization's money and when we were done nothing changed, although suspicion now focused on the Safety Department (obviously inept!). Eventually we got smart enough to ask the performers if they knew the risks – yes they did – it's a cumulative disorder. Did they know the exposures – yes, that equipment puts out 95 decibels. Did they know how to use their protective equipment – yes and here's how to use them! So what's the issue? Oh, people just don't wear them. Aha!! Not a "can't do" issue, but a "won't do" issue - a performance management problem that training wouldn't fix.

After that we'd refuse to do the requested training when it didn't appear to be the problem (often under threat that our futures could be "freed up"). Instead we offered to train supervisors on how to get compliance with existing standards – and that worked.

The classic map of Performance Analysis was articulated by Robert F. Mager and Peter Pipe in *Analyzing Performance Problems or You Really Oughta Wanna* (1984). You really oughta take a longer look at it or alternate sources.

Task Analysis

Once a training problem is confirmed we need to know what a given task demands in terms of knowledge and skills. So a <u>Task Analysis</u> is required.

Traditional task analysis identifies the input (how do you know when to initiate the task) and outputs (how do you know when it's done), the tools or aids required, the standard for how well it must be done (see Chapter 2, What's the Issue?) and under what **Conditions** (Context).

Task analysis then breaks a task down into its steps and asks what skills and knowledge are required at each step to perform the task. The output of this will be the input for learning objectives and lesson plans.

Consider learning to change a flat tire and how our discussion of context comes into play. If we train people to change a flat on a sunny day in the parking lot, they do *not* learn how to do it in the dark, in heavy traffic, on a curve in the road, or in the rain or snow. Learning objectives must reference the performance, the standards (how well) and the conditions (context) to prepare performers for the real world they will face.

Another common example involves people being taught to do a circle check on a piece of equipment. Good as far as it goes. Yet inspection checklists often omit the standards needed. The "hydraulic hose" or "fire extinguisher" references on a check box may not include which things to look for in each of those items. Standards added to the back of the inspection form help.

If we expect people to not just do a circle check but to actually troubleshoot any problems they find, then the conditions of our training must change along these lines: "Given a demo, a copy of the procedure, a checklist and a piece of equipment that has been disabled in 3 ways, you will identify the deficiencies, determine which require operator or maintenance interventions, and recommend actions to the satisfaction of the instructor."

The learning that you get is strongly influenced by how well you craft learning outcomes that include conditions, performance and standards as identified by a task analysis.

Task Analysis is the insertion point where Standards and Context get built into the system.

Whoa, wait a minute. The reference to the elements of Task Analysis a few paragraphs back went by pretty fast. And what's with the **BOLD** face on "**Conditions**"?

Look out!! Here comes a BIGGIE.

To prepare for the next example, stop reading and view Martin Bromiley's video "Just a Routine Operation." https://www.youtube.com/watch?v=JzlvgtPlof4&t=7s

Bromiley's 14 minute video re-enacts his wife's "routine" surgery. During the procedure she stops breathing and the anaesthetists lose situational awareness while repeatedly trying to intubate her. After finally stabilizing her oxygen levels they decide to cancel the operation and leave her to wake up and recover on her own. She never does and succumbs days later.

As the anaesthetists worked, the OR nurses try unsuccessfully to nudge the doctors to initiate an available procedure which is well known for this type of situation.

Even though standards were clear and professionals were well-trained and well-intentioned, "sh*t happened".

Health care is a unique environment. Hospitals often have two hierarchies. One in which doctors answer to a Chief Medical Officer who reports to the hospital Board and another in which everyone else answers through the management structure to the CEO who also reports to the Board. When there is an issue or conflict between a doctor and a nurse the first "official" level of authority that bridges between the two is at the Board level. Obviously deference to the Board is impossible in the midst of a dispute.

But if management authority must shift from management control to frontline expertise when we change contexts from Routine to Non-Routine to Emergencies, then what should the nurses have done? What standards, procedures and authority prevail when a frontline person is aware that someone over whom they have no authority is behaving inappropriately and/or making an error?

Our Task Analyses and the resultant training plans and procedures are often aimed at "hard" tasks – change the pump, operate the equipment, or monitor the system. But when we do the "soft skills" tasks – lead, motivate, plan or coordinate – things get fuzzier. And they do so for good reason. When we add the element of human interaction with all of its individual and group complexities, we face conditions that are more numerous, more widely variable and subject to rapid change.

There is little need to point out the potential consequences of errors in health care.

Here in Ontario, where the author lives, a *National Post* article by Tom Blackwell (January 16, 2015) reported that researchers estimate there will be 72,000 medical errors and 3,500 to 9,000 deaths related to medical error per year in this Canadian province of 13.4 million people. Considering the vast number of health care interventions that would occur annually in a population of that number, the error estimate may well only represent a miniscule percentage. However, during 2013 only 29 events and 6 deaths were reported. That being in a province where medical errors must be disclosed to the patient but where responsibility to report those same errors to the College of Physicians, the hospital or the Ministry of Health is unclear.

In the United States statistics suggest that the number deaths due to medical errors and hospital acquired infections far exceed annual deaths by workplace or motor vehicle accidents combined. (Max, 2009)

So why are Conditions such an issue when doing Task Analysis?

During the Bromiley operation the conditions (context) rapidly moved from Routine to Non-Routine to Emergency. As such, standards and procedures had to change on the fly. So too the authority limits of the frontline performers, including both doctors and nurses, had to change particularly in regard to identifying and taking action when peers were not acknowledging or responding to shifting contexts.

And health care does not have a monopoly on such examples that could be anticipated in a Task Analysis.

To be proactively prepared for error events, the Task Analysis and it's training and procedural outcomes have to anticipate that differing conditions (Routine versus Non-Routine versus Emergencies) need *separate analyses*. These in turn will change the other elements of the Task Analysis (inputs, outputs, standards, steps, knowledge and skills needed).

During complex human interactions in situations of changing context, issues of power and authority, professional and organizational culture, effective communication and maintenance of situational awareness all land on the table.

Our choice is to either prepare ourselves proactively through robust applications of "What's the Issue" and of Task Analysis or wait until "sh*t happens" and then do it reactively.

Although it's not possible to foresee every eventuality and prepare for them, proactivity is still both preferred and professionally responsible.

Now, a few more words on some Task Analysis variations.

Job Safety Analysis (JSA)

Job Safety Analysis is one of the most searched safety terms on the net. A JSA is required in many jurisdictions and organizations. A JSA is identical to a Task Analysis in identifying inputs, outputs, tools, conditions, standards and steps. But from there on they differ from Task Analysis in that they don't ask what skills and knowledge are needed (the stuff that lesson plans are built on). Instead they ask, What are the risks or hazards at each step of the task? Then a JSA produces *procedures* with built-in controls to reduce risk.

Because the JSA focusses on the risks and not the required skills and knowledge, training based solely on procedures derived from a JSA <u>may not necessarily include all of the skills and knowledge requirements</u>. This can leave the trainer and the organization with their due diligence hanging out.

When asked after an error event, "How did you determine what to teach them?" a reference to comprehensive Task Analysis, not just a JSA or a procedure, is the best defense.

Cognitive Task Analysis

Recent work on reliable performance in high-risk environments, particularly in emergency response situations, has produced Cognitive Task Analysis. How do we capture the stuff inside the head of that experienced performer before they retire? The stuff that comes from years of experience and that others don't seem to have learned or mastered? How does that seasoned equipment operator know by sound or touch what is happening beyond the range of sight or sensors? How does that fire commander know amidst chaos, ambiguity and incomplete information whether to attack or withdraw?

Such is the territory of Cognitive Task Analysis. It's particularly suited for application to Non-Routine and Emergency situations.

In this case the techniques are quite different from traditional Task Analysis and Job Safety Analysis. Processes such as "cognitive maps for knowledge elicitation" and "incident based Cognitive Task Analysis" are used.

And if your organization is headed towards greater integration of Artificial Intelligence systems (AI) then consider that the outputs (learnings) from Cognitive Task Analysis will be critical inputs to AI systems. Such systems will be able to process inputs, variables and options before and beyond what human operators can, provide tools, and free operators and professionals, particularly in Non-Routine and Emergency situations, to make better decisions in the face of increasingly complex challenges.

For more, check out *Working Minds – A Practitioner's Guide to Cognitive Task Analysis* by Crandall, Klein, and Hoffman.

Back to the Training Design Cycle.

Learner Assessment

If our Task Analysis identified 10 things that a learner needs to know or do, then we can ask them to demonstrate their competence explaining and doing those things. If they already know 5 of the 10 things, then we've identified the 5 other things that our training needs to focus on - we've done our Learner Assessment.

Curriculum Development

Having identified the learning needs we proceed to Curriculum Development – Learning Objectives, Lesson Plans, Training Techniques, and Training/Learning Aids (Audiovisuals, manuals).

Pilot and Revision

If we're preparing training to be delivered to a large chunk of the work population, it's prudent to run a pilot program first, iron out the bugs and revise to produce the final training program.

Deliver and Evaluate

Finally, we deliver the program and evaluate. Ideally the evaluation should involve the 4 levels articulated by Donald Kirkpatrick (https://www.kirkpatrickpartners.com):

- Reaction (the proverbial smile sheet)
- Learning (to match the Learning Objectives)
- Behaviour on the Job (to confirm performance)
- Organizational Results (to link training to organizational goals).

And then the Cycle begins anew.

If, for example, a trainer is to teach First Aid, they have probably been certified to do so by an agency like the Red Cross. The Standards, Task Analysis, Lesson Plans, Materials, and Evaluation formats have been provided and all the trainer needs to do is deliver and assess. But when the same trainer is asked to "take care of the training" regarding a new procedure, piece of equipment or regulation, how much of the Training Design Cycle are they responsible for? The Performance Analysis? The Task Analysis? The Learner Assessment? The Curriculum Development? And are they expected to do so on top of their regular duties. This is a situation that's more common than you might think.

Training design and delivery literally shapes the performance that your organization can deliver in Routine, Non-Routine and Emergency situations.

How's your organization doing?

For starters use Performance Analysis (or What's the Issue?) to determine if the issues you face are training problems or something else.

Then take Task Analysis seriously in its various forms and apply it, at the very least, to the different contexts of Routine, Non-Routine and Emergencies. Task Analysis can represent a big commitment in time and resources, but the payoffs in terms of performance, productivity, clarity and reduced risk will far exceed that initial investment. Task Analysis by necessity needs to involve experienced performers. In so doing, a better product is produced and ownership of the outcomes increases.

When tools such as MindManager Mind Map Software by Mindjet, a visual work management solution, are used (highly recommended), job incumbents can be encouraged to initiate on-going updates to the Task Analyses. This in turn develops more ownership and sets the direction towards a Self-Correcting Organization.

Yet sometimes, despite our best efforts, our thoughtful designs and our best intentions, "sh*t happens". What then?

Let's shift our focus to Recovering from Error.

PART 2

RECOVERING FROM ERROR

CHAPTER 4

THE HAZARDS OF TRADITIONAL INVESTIGATION

So what's the problem with what we've been doing? Haven't error rates dropped substantially over time?

Of course they have. Tremendous progress has been made through better technology, work practices, legislation, awareness, and protective equipment.

Yet many organizations experience a plateau in their progress. That mirrors our experience with fitness pursuits. When we're out of shape and start to exercise we make fast gains but eventually reach a point where that rate of gain slows down. Then, to get that extra distance in our jump or extra seconds off of our time, we have to pay closer attention to the finer details of our performance.

In the workplace the finer details that give those extra gains have to do with human performance and particularly with our response to error events. Paying closer attention to investigation gives us the leverage and the mechanism to make those gains.

Motivation is well served when we both acknowledge those things we need to move away from *and* set forward looking goals. So to start, here are the investigation practices we need to shed.

NOTE: You can use this as a checklist of what to avoid. If you already buy into the idea that current practices are lacking, move onto Chapter 5.

Hindsight bias

Sydney Dekker in *The Field Guide to Understanding Risk* (2006) highlights "hindsight bias" as *the* major problem with investigations. Hindsight bias rears its ugly head as soon as the "should" or "could have" references comes out, as in "What should you have done?" or "What could you have done to prevent this?"

These hypothetical questions imply that you *should have* foreseen the outcome that was about to happen. You should have been able to see the future. And you *should have* adjusted accordingly. Of course that's impossible.

People do what they think is right in the moment based on the circumstances at hand.

Even in employment interviews hypothetical questions only generate hypothetical answers aimed to please the interviewer. Behavior description questions on the other hand identify a candidate's typical behaviors. Investigation requires the same focus. Get the story, not conjecture!

Avoid the fiction of hindsight bias! Stick with the truth about what happened. "How did it make perfect sense to do what you did, or did not do, in that context at that time?"

Investigator/Investigation bias

"That was his third incident this year. I think we all know what the cause is."

"That's a maintenance problem, not something we in operations did."

"We, the manufacturer, say that operator error is the problem."

"If management would spend more money this wouldn't be happening."

These and an infinite variety of other rationalizations represent the biases that creep into investigation. They are the causal assumptions that we make as opposed to the facts of what is.

Each of us comes from a context and a background of specific experience. The investigator must acknowledge that their own assumptions and first impressions can throw them off course. Regularly ask yourself: "How do I know that? What's the evidence? If I probe more will that assumption still hold up?" Be suspicious of the accuracy of simplistic assignments of cause particularly in complex multivariate situations.

Our investigations themselves can also be biased by the models of causation that we embrace or by report forms that reflect those models and direct attention in specific but sometimes misleading ways.

Overgeneralization

Because of a surprising limitation in conscious brain capacity that we'll talk more about later, we have a tendency to generalize.

Teenagers do it best. Why do you want to go there? "Cause everyone's going there." Why are you doing that? "Cause everyone's doing it." What do you want one of those for? "Cause everyone has one. (Or everyone's doing that.)" Why do you want one of those? "Everyone has one." Those teenage generalizations often relate to the pull of group dynamics and to the desire to establish identity.

In investigations our tendency to generalize can have us seeing bigger patterns in, what are often, unique events. After all, we are pattern-seeking creatures by nature.

It's not unusual to hear groaning amongst a workforce after an incident when everyone gets retrained - as if the incident represented a system-wide problem. Maybe it's only an individual performance issue. You can always ask for demonstrations of competence to determine the scope of a suspected competence issue. But to train beyond the scale of the occurrence will waste time and money. Overgeneralization at its worst!

Use of questionable causation models

Over the last century the field of incident investigation, particularly in the area of workplace injuries, has seen the evolution of a variety of causation models - domino theories, multiple causation, Swiss cheese and so on.

In their time these models served our thinking well and contributed to a robust prevention movement. Recently many of these have been subject to more critical scrutiny. Books like Fred Manuele's *Heinrich Revisited* (2002) and Paul Difford's *Redressing the Balance: a Commonsense Approach to Causation* (2011) cast shadows across those historical perspectives.

Related to these concerns is an ongoing bias in older models that tilts towards an Aristotelian view of cause and effect. Here again this approach has served us well in regard to physical systems in which *causal* analysis is a primary and invaluable tool. However, in the complex world of human performance with free will, human fallibility, competing goals, constrained resources, and group dynamics, a more Einsteinian view of the *relatedness* of things makes much more sense. A different approach to understanding error causation will be offered in Chapter 6.

Use of inappropriate questions

Because our brains are literal and our attention follows where it's directed, the structure and type of questions that we use shapes the answers and explanations we get back. Whether these come from questionable causation models or clumsiness in language use, inappropriate questions can limit the accuracy and completeness of the information we receive and lead us to ill-formed conclusions.

"Loaded" questions that generate a hindsight bias and the inappropriate use of "Why?" (more on that shortly) serve to divert our attention from more useful inquiry.

Damaging presuppositions

The safety field has been plagued by a series of presuppositions or assumptions presented in the form of slogans that have shaped beliefs and gone largely unchallenged. These include the following:

- "Safety is Job 1."
- "Is it safe?"
- "All accidents are preventable."
- "Our goal is Zero injuries."

Just how these slogans cause damage will be fully explained in Chapter 5.

Not treating investigation as an organizational intervention

Every question in an organization is an intervention with the potential to change the organization.

As mentioned in the Introduction, asking "What can we do to make things better around here?" without appropriate follow-up can lead to an "I don't care" response the next time we ask. We shape the reality of how people experience us as individuals and the organization through our actions with each encounter.

Investigation by its nature is loaded with questions aimed at discovering what happened and what should change. These significant organizational interventions are often led by harried frontline supervisors and treated as a "pain in the ass" activity to be gotten over with as quickly as possible and with the least amount of time and effort.

Yet investigation is a powerful tool intended to achieve continuous improvement. Instead, what if it were treated as an opportunity to open a window on how we operate? What if we engaged it as a learning event to continually adapt our work and work culture?

<u>Weak follow-up</u>

Investigation recommendations sputter when they're not followed up on diligently. Once we identify behaviors that need changing, the action often stops at "Be more careful."

Confirming or reiterating the standard of what's wanted is just the beginning.

Behavior change requires increased activity on the part of an immediate supervisor and their manager in turn. Coaching, follow-up, job observation, and skills acquisition are all needed along with the attendant time commitment that these activities require.

But recommendations are often made without a realistic acknowledgement of supervisor's availability to adequately deliver on such follow-ups.

Not having the right people in the room

An incident occurs at 3 am. The supervisor, whose week will end at 8 am that morning (along with that of his or her crew), rushes to get a report in (required within 24 hours) and involve the people available at hand.

The next morning recommendations turn up on a maintenance manager's desk. That person was not involved in the investigation and has only the brief account outlined in the report to go on. Since the recommendations don't quite make sense, they are added to the bottom of the pile of 300 items already awaiting attention. And there they sit.

Months later a follow-up inquiry comes along and the report is brought back out only for the manager to proclaim that it's really an engineering issue. The report is forwarded along so it can sit at the bottom of the Engineering Department list for another wait. And so it goes.

Alternately we can get an initial report out to satisfy the reporting deadline, then wait if need be, until we can get the supervisor, the workers involved, Maintenance,

Engineering and whomever else may be required and resolve the issue in one session.

Get the right people in the room.

Correlation/causation confusion

So I guess cancer may not make me better looking after all, although I'm sticking to the delusion if only for purposes of self-image. But it remains an example of correlation/causation confusion.

Any model of "causation" that implies a linear cause/effect may well have validity in machine/equipment systems where processes literally work in a linear fashion. And although it's easy to be seduced by "This is his fourth incident this year, we know the cause", people systems are anything but linear and straightforward. They are complex, interrelated, not necessarily rational and influenced by a multitude of personal, social, organizational and non-work factors. Once more, think like Einstein and relativity rather than Aristotle and cause/effect.

Compulsion to do something

I'm always struck by the compulsion to do something or else it's implied that I don't believe in prevention. Really?

Best-laid plans often go awry. No matter how carefully a project is planned, something may still go wrong. Our standards can be clear and reasonable. People can understand their responsibilities and how to do their jobs. They can comply with standards and have the resources to get the job done. And still "sh*t" happens!

But how do we respond? Do we launch massive re-training programs, create unnecessary additional procedures or over-scrutinize well-intentioned and responsible workers?

Why? Maybe our systems are OK. Maybe a thorough investigation is enough to acknowledge the uniqueness of an event and simply move on.

Am I afraid that something *must* be done - or else it reflects on me? Such reactions often overcomplicate our systems and make it more difficult to reach our goals.

Loss of situation awareness during investigation

A loss of situational awareness is often associated with failure incidents. It's regularly mentioned in high-risk activities like aviation, power generation and health care. Has our training installed situation awareness in our operators and professionals so that their responses under pressure become more appropriate?

Investigation is not immune to this loss of situational awareness. Is it squeezed in on top of a myriad of other tasks? Done under a deadline? Viewed as an obligation to be gotten out of the way? Done by investigators who conduct these important interventions while in less than optimal states of mind?

Trapped by the confines of the form/format

Many investigation forms or formats are based on a causation model. Does the form have a section labeled "Causation" or "Causal Factors" or "Contributing Factors"? Do "Unsafe Acts or Conditions" or "Root Cause(s)" regularly turn up as sub-headings?

When a form lists the possible causes or contributors in a checklist, should the form's author include six choices or six hundred? If we only list a few, will the investigator's attention move beyond that list to include items that have been left out? If we use a blank form, will they have the enough prompts to ask appropriate questions?

We are asking the form to do too much!

Use the form to collect information, document physical evidence, and report witness statements. Do *not* include a section on causation or the investigator will be tempted to seek causation information at the same time as they interview witnesses. This will contaminate the data collection process – more on this later as well.

Ignorance or non-acknowledgement of the culture or context

Significantly missing from many forms - and hence from questioning - is an inquiry into the work context. What's it like to work at this organization? In this department? For that supervisor or manager? How were you feeling that day? What pressures does the work group put on a person working here?

These significant influences on human behavior have an important bearing on what people consider "normal" behavior.

<u>Non-acceptance of paradox and complexity</u>

Using linear or rigid causation models to explain how the world works does little to acknowledge the true complexity of people, work interactions and systems.

Individuals are complex enough all on their own. Work dynamics add even more complexity. Throw in conflicting goals, constrained resources, deadline or budget pressures, worry over issues at home, strained relationships within the workplace, uncertainty and, well, you get the picture.

If you look for simple causes in a dynamic, changing environment, you may find naive solutions.

People regularly embrace paradox in ways that defy logic. Well intentioned, devoted workers may bend standards that are not designed to cover every unique situation for very logical reasons and without violating their personal commitment to safety, respect or environment. If they genuinely try to solve a problem when no other guidance is available, should they be "blamed" for a negative outcome?

<u>Raising the "blame" card</u>

As we'll discuss later on, our approach to investigation and in particular our verbal and non-verbal communication patterns can send unintended messages of blame.

Once a well-intentioned worker senses that an "honest" error leads to blame and possible punishment, all the bets are off in terms of any willing reporting of the circumstances. Our ability to get to the facts and achieve prevention drastically diminishes.

Lack of visual techniques

Too often investigators restrict themselves to verbal discussion amongst themselves to determine causation. Talking isn't enough for listeners to grasp the whole picture. Our ability to juggle multiple variables in our head or to do so verbally is limited.

So what do we do? Go visual, with pictures and pictorials, with diagrams and listings of variables, and with representations of relationships between factors. All are essential aids to witnesses, investigators and learning teams.

Use paper, screen shots, flip charts, white boards, sticky notes, whatever's at hand. Visual techniques will also help to foster a collective understanding and acceptance of conclusions within group settings.

When in doubt - go visual, go visual, go visual!

Phew!

So I guess the "state of the art" isn't so "artful" after all.

Enough of what to avoid, where do we go from here?

CHAPTER 5

PRESUPPOSITIONS AND GENERAL PRINCIPLES

Here are some useful ways of thinking about investigation.

Consider **highlighting** or <u>underlining</u> any passages that resonate with you.

<u>Presuppositions</u>

All language presupposes meaning of some kind.

Yet some phrases imply or assume meaning or truth that's questionable. The safety profession in particular has been plagued by catch phrases and slogans that simply don't work.

Let's examine a generic example, then some safety specific ones.

<u>Can I help?</u>

How natural to ask of someone entering your office - "How can I help you?" Yet think about what's presupposed. "How can *I* help you?" implies you must be the helper. So *they* must be the one who is "helpless" and you must be in charge of the helping process. A one-way ticket to dependency.

In retail they've figured out that asking a clerk for help just irritates customers who don't want to be dependent on someone else to find what they want. More recently you hear them ask "Are you finding everything you need today?"

Next time try "What's up?" instead of "How can I help you?" - no dependency implied. Let's grow independent self-correcting people.

Safety is job 1

If only I had a dollar for every time I've heard that one. If safety is job 1, then what's the best that production or service or environment or quality can be? Since 1 is an ordinal reference everything else must be of lesser importance. So when a supervisor says 'We have to focus on production today", they get the response "Well, obviously you don't believe in safety." Conflict has been created where none was needed.

How about this instead: "Around here safety, production, service, quality, environment - these are all important and we have to figure out how to balance them appropriately"?

Avoid pitting major functions against each other with the "number 1" reference.

Is it safe?

Sounds like a reasonable question right? But you probably learned in grade school that any question with some form of the verb "to be" in it is a "yes/no" question. Only one of two answers is available.

Safety is not a yes/no issue and never has been.

At the very least it is a balance between three factors - Cost, Risk and Benefit. It's OK to ask if a Risk Assessment has been done and if the risk is acceptable or not. And it's OK to ask if a Cost/Benefit Analysis of the recommendations has been done to choose the best alternative. But if you ask "Is it safe?" you're asking for an opinion, any response is correct.

As an example, consider the person who has been up and down ladders thousands of times in their life, correctly positioned it, maintained a center of balance, carefully ascended and descended, but seldom had another hold the base and yet they've never fallen. Their repeat behavioral reality has "taught" them that they can successfully climb a ladder without someone else holding it.

Now they come to work at your organization with your rule to only climb a ladder when the base is held. One day they walk a distance across the facility carrying a ladder to do a simple five-minute job. But they forget to bring someone to hold the ladder. They set it up, check to see if anyone is looking, ascend and do the job just as you, their supervisor, round the corner and ask "Is that safe?" They think back on all their life experience and say "Absolutely." (After all you did ask them for their opinion, right?) Then you give them three days off without pay and wonder why you don't get much cooperation from them from that point on.

At the very least you could have said "That violates our standards and there's a consequence for that." The consequence would be taken with much better grace than being punished for having a different opinion about how safe is safe.

"0" is the useful goal

Really? What does a perfectionistic and perhaps unsustainable goal do for motivation? Imagine meeting monthly to report on safety statistics that confirm we weren't perfect again this month. But don't fret we'll do it again next month and rub your noses in your imperfection again. (These are called safety meetings by the way.)

"0" leads to a culture of perfectionism where error tolerance is also usually "0."

Not useful.

Even those remarkable organizations that have achieved zero injuries for a while, have struggled to sustain that performance over time.

Perfection has no stamina. It doesn't last.

How about simply shooting for continuous improvement to lower frequency and severity rates?

All accidents are preventable

Ah, the granddaddy of damaging presuppositions!

In our workshops I frequently ask "How many of you believe that *all* accidents are preventable?" Few, if any, hands are ever raised. Then I ask "How many of you think that despite our best efforts and our good intentions, occasionally "Sh*t happens?" All the hands are raised.

Any leader who stands up and says "All accidents are preventable" flies in the face of practically everyone's real world experience. Comments like this severely diminish his or her credibility.

And if all accidents are preventable, then we must be able to control everything - ground conditions, weather, people's state of mind, where they direct their attention, even their motivation! "All accidents are preventable" should be referred to as the "God Delusion" of the safety profession – that's who you'd have to be to control all of that!

Finally, if all accidents are preventable and I have an accident, most people tend to think, well I guess it's my fault, I'm to blame. When we feel blamed or at fault we don't open up with complete honesty to seek prevention, particularly if we think some punishment is coming or that our organization is not error tolerant.

So put all of that "sh*t" out of your head!

General Principles (that do work)

Here are some principles or assumptions that are much more useful, keeping in mind that all generalizations are lies, including this one.

You get the people you deserve

The people around us, our children or peers, subordinates or life mates, all bring their own mix of personality, biases, and behaviors to any situation. Of course we don't "deserve" the employee from hell that we inherited and who should have been dealt with years ago. Yet at the same time we get the people we deserve to the degree that we shape the way others experience both us and the organization. Many behaviors that we encounter are a response to the reality that they have experienced. And what they experience depends partly on the way we have framed it for them.

Here's a few examples: Transparency, Tonal Shifts, and Investigation Experience.

Transparency

A supervisor gets called into their manager's office only to be told that a new procedure or process has been adopted. Since this sounds like the stupidest thing that he or she has ever heard, they do their best to get the manager to reconsider, only to learn that the decision is made and that it's not up for grabs. The supervision, knowing full well what kind of reaction this news will generate from their department or crew, gloomily heads off to deliver the news. Sure enough, the reaction is vocal and negative, culminating with the question, "And whose stupid idea was this anyway?" The poor supervisor, all too often, responds, "Well, it was the manager's idea."

The supervisor has chosen the easy path and taken themselves off the "hot seat" by saying that he or she is not to blame. They have instead, become "transparent", a pane of glass through which the apparent stupidity of the boss can be seen. Unfortunately, in that instant they have destroyed respect within the organization. Why would anyone respect orders from an apparently impotent supervisor? Why go around them to their manager, the source of the stupidity? In fact, why would anyone put out much of an effort in an organization run by a bunch of fools?

I've worked in organizations with thousands of employees where everyone thought the managers were a bunch of idiots. Where did they get this idea? They don't sit in meetings where management makes choices between difficult alternatives. Employees get that idea from leaders, middle managers, supervisors, and professionals who opted for the short-term gain of being blameless, while contributing to the long-term degradation of respect within the organization. Needless to say, subsequent messages from managers so tagged get tainted with the same negativity.

The alternative is to "take the hit." When people start to complain, explain that the decision is made, who made it is not the issue, and here's how we'll proceed from now on. (More on how to do this without being "shot" as the messenger, later on.) The person representing the organization must visibly "buy in" to the decision, and not sabotage it by becoming transparent.

This is no different from the parent who tells his teenager to be in by 11:00. Then, when the teenager complains and says "Gee all the other kids get to stay out later, you don't really want me to be in by 11:00, do you?" The parent answers, "Well, I'd let you stay out later, but your Mom..." Why then, be surprised when the teenager now begins to play one parent off against the other. Few of us can honestly say we've never been transparent.

So we shape the reality of how people experience our organizations and, in great part then, we get the people we deserve.

Tonal shifts

Simple tonal shifts also make huge differences.

With my child I say, (excitedly) "Hey, wanna go outside and play some ball?" Lo and behold the child not only wants to, but learns to anticipate and enjoy that activity. Two hours later I say to the same child, (in a hang dog, dejected kind of tone) "Well, it's time to do your homework." and the child immediately objects. It doesn't take many exposures to those different ways of non-verbally "framing" the different activities before the child has been "programmed" to like playing ball and to hate doing homework because of the associations they carry. What reality would I shape if I used the same excited tone to describe homework that I used for playing ball?

In the workplace it goes like this: In one breath we talk with anticipation about it being Friday afternoon and "only a couple of hours 'til we get out of here." Later, in a bored monotone, we announce that it's time for the staff meeting. Then we wonder why our people can't wait to go home but dread the next meeting.

The good news, of course, is that our own behavior is something we can control. Thus the way that others experience the organization, at least as they do so through us as a point of contact is also within our control.

Investigation experience

As we've already pointed out, every question in an organization is an intervention that changes the organization.

And how we treat errors will signal to others how they are likely to be treated as well. This seemingly innocent activity, the investigation of incidents, has enormous power to create positive workplace cultures or to taint them irreparably.

- Some Useful Investigation Principles

Consider these investigation specific principles:

- To err is human.
  Thank you, Lucio Anneo Seneca (4 BC – 65 AD), for reminding us so succinctly of our humanity.

- No one *intends* to make an error unless they have serious personal issues.
  Assume that most, but not necessarily all, people are well-intentioned.

- No two situations are the same.
  When infinitely variable humans bring their differing experiences to dynamic workplace situations, every incident is distinctly unique.

- All situations involve multiple variables.
  Pursuing a single root cause or asking "What's *the* cause?" just doesn't cut it.

- The conscious mind has a limited capacity to process multiple variables without the use of visual tools and representations.
  Go visual, go visual, go visual when dealing with complexity. Make it your mantra.

- People naturally delete, distort and generalize information. Related to the limited firepower at the conscious level, we constantly delete, distort and generalize. We don't do this on purpose, but simply as a function of normal communication and brain processing. Our investigation techniques must both acknowledge this and enable us to overcome it. Our job is to recover deleted information.

- All organizations present conflicting goals to performers in resource constrained environments.
No surprise here, but another layer of complexity gets added to the stack.

- All actions/non-actions/assessments are considered normal by the performer in the context of the situation. What we do always seems like the right thing at that time and in that context. It just seems reasonable.

- Perfection is unlikely and pursuit of it (zero injuries or errors) is damaging.
Enough said.

- Recovery is more important than perfection.
Ah, Michael Grinder's essential insight. Seek to recover quicker, to return to a state of normal operations. The organizations and the people that do so thrive.

- Self-correcting systems are preferred.
Seek solutions that install learning systems and self-correcting processes rather than one-up responses.

- Perceptions of error forgiveness are crucial.
Not only must we be error tolerant, we must be perceived that way.

CHAPTER 6

THE LAST CAUSATION MODEL YOU'LL EVER NEED

As you've read, cause/effect thinking is an Aristotelian artifact. In the complex environment of the workplace it's impractical to apply the scientific method in everyday use - to hold all dependent variables constant so as to study the independent one.

Instead, we need to understand the relationships between the variables. Yet it is hard to approach the workplace in an Einsteinian manner, acknowledging relativity, because workplace investigation forms and formats are loaded with language that biases their questions towards those linear causation models of the past.

The most damaging aspect of the cause/effect approach is it's constant companion "Why?". "Why?" is useful in tracing back issues in mechanical and equipment systems, but only until you get to the human component.

When you hear "Why?" or it's variations "Why did you do that?" "What were you thinking?" you've entered what's called the "Blame Frame". See *Don't Ask Why?!* (Smith-Chong, 1991) and *Do You Know How Another Knows To Be?* (Smith-Chong, 2017).

The sequence of the Chongs' Blame Frame goes like this:

- **Why** is a linguistic device to establish explanation or reason based on the cause/effect model wherein y causes x.

- "Why" leads to "**Should**" which comes from expectation or entitlement – "What should you have done?" "This is how it should be." "I should be the CEO. I've got a degree." "He or she shouldn't be doing this to me."

- If there's a "Should" then there must be a "**Right or Wrong**".

- And with "Right and Wrong" there must be a "**Justification**" for any variation from the "right" way.

- Of course when you've done "wrong", along comes "**Guilt, Fault, and Blame**".

- And those who make such a judgement can support a sense of "**Self-Importance, Self-Esteem and Ego**".

- So they can "**Avoid Responsibility**" because it's the perpetrator who's to blame for the problem.

And all this stems from the assumption of "causality" instead of relatedness.

It becomes a self-reinforcing loop that stifles further learning and development. Some organizations actually encourage people to ask "Why?" five or six times in a row to "get to the bottom of things." Yike!

The Chongs, by the way, offer a brilliant alternative – The Freedom Frame. Some questions from it are incorporated into Chapter 9 on Interviewing.

Another phenomenon occurs when investigators ask, "What is *the* root cause?" Inevitably the investigator's bias will create the cause. (See "Investigator/Investigation Bias" in Chapter 4.)

Assuming that people need to be "fixed", particularly with punishment, **does not work** when people make honest errors. Thinking that another needs fixing wrongly presupposes that people must be broken. Most are not.

REMEMBER: <u>You cannot punish your way out of error.</u>
(Bob Edwards's conference presentation –
ENFORM, Banff Alberta, 2015)

We can, however, fine tune a system and deal with behaviours.

<u>The Last Causation Model You'll Ever Need</u>

The Principles cited in the last chapter, the imperative to avoid "Why?", and cause/effect thinking push us to this alternative:

<u>Phillips' Law of Human Performance</u>

**Well-intentioned people
facing competing organizational and personal goals
in environments of constrained resources
occasionally and unconsciously
make errors of attention, perception, and judgment.**

And this is NORMAL.

In other words:

*Sh*t Happens*

And <u>*how*</u> you respond and recover is
what makes all the difference.

Let's break that down.

"Well-intentioned people"

It seems obvious that few, if any, people come in to work in the morning planning or expecting to make an error or to hurt themselves or someone else. Those who do so probably have a mental health issue of some sort. Most folks are well intentioned.

"facing competing organizational and personal goals"

Organizational goals present their own conflicts amongst themselves – speed versus quality versus cost versus safety versus service. When we're told that "everything is important" or that something, such as safety, is "job 1", we set ourselves up for a multitude of interpretations and potential conflict. Then we add personal goals. The complexity thickens when our experience, values or beliefs do not match what the organization wants.

In many organizations general goals are promoted as values or beliefs – safety, quality, customer first, environment, and so on. Were you to present such a list to a group of organization members most would probably agree that those things are worthy targets. But when offered in general terms, they end up being interesting but not always useful. We all believe in safety for instance but if we poll a group regarding any specific safety issue, what should the speed limit be on Street X, for example, we'll get a spectrum of answers. Perceptions of how safe is safe in any given situation will be as varied as the number of people you ask. And that bag of perceptions can produce conflict when organizational standards are poorly defined.

"in environments of constrained resources"

When facing constrained resources - time, budget, people, equipment, materials, information, authority – we get our noses rubbed in the reasonableness of the standards we've set to support our goals. And as we now know, reasonableness changes whenever our operating circumstances change.

In the work place well-intentioned people simply strive to get the job done, often, with choices that are not covered in the manual or the procedure. They're not covered because current goal conflicts and resource constraints are not written into the manual or the procedure or the training. You could try writing standards and procedures for everything anyone might ever encounter but your career may not be long enough. And your operations can become procedure bound. People wait for you to tell them what to do next and for you to produce a procedure. So you defeat the very goals you set out to achieve – to be profitable, or safe or efficient.

Work groups benefit from honest and regular (i.e. daily) reviews of current operating circumstances. Only then can standards be adjusted to address the current situation. In most operations circumstances are constantly changing - on evenings, on weekends, during financial challenges, or during any unusual demand on resources.

Because we can't foresee everything, the individual performer needs to be given authority limits to address the unforeseen that require an immediate response. Training to respond and problem solve through simulations and scenarios run in real time are more useful than more procedures.

Consider too that how we respond to the individual who steps up to take action in the moment to address an issue, regardless the outcome, defines our culture. Do we promote or discourage such initiative? Under which circumstances?

"occasionally and unconsciously"

"Occasionally" making errors may be more or less unacceptable depending on the frequency and how it compares to historic or expected norms.

"Unconsciously" is the kicker. The unconscious seems to be the big gun, whirring away in the background and hosting our beliefs, temperaments, attitudes, instincts, decision strategies and information storage. For example, I'm right-handed and usually reach for a cup or a doorknob with my right hand. I don't consciously choose to do so. It just happens (unconsciously). I could practice 'til I was almost ambidextrous but if you threw a ball at me I'd probably still reach up with my right hand (unconsciously).

In situations of conflicting goals and constrained resources, well-intentioned people regularly make unconscious choices in the moment because it's perceived to be the right thing to do given the information and resources that the person has available to them at the time.

To make a conscious decision to err, to do so willfully, excludes the performer from our description of "well-intentioned" and is not what is going on in most error situations. Although malicious action is always a possibility, most errors involve a large unconscious component.

"make errors of attention, perception, and judgment."

Sometimes we are distracted, or overwhelmed by information. Sometimes we get fixated on only a few aspects of the information environment to the exclusion of the rest.

Sometimes we lack the experience, training or information to understand and discriminate amongst data and data patterns. Sometimes analysis and decision-making strategies are unavailable or inadequate for the current situation or they're misapplied.

So, as you review "Phillips' Law of Human Performance", notice that blaming well-intentioned performers who, in the face of conflicting goals and constrained resources, made an error that seems inappropriate in hindsight is an act devoid of reality. It's conjectural and not factual to what the person actually experienced because it's based on hindsight (What should or could you have done?). And blaming well-intentioned people for being normal (To Err is Human after all) and for trying to solve a problem in the face of ambiguity sends the worst message possible. It reduces the chance of getting factual accounts of what was actually experienced.

In *Pre-Accident Investigations.* (Conklin, 2012) Todd Conklin suggests let's commit to moving from a "crime and punishment model" to a "diagnose and treat" model of managing human performance.

Good advice.

Now let's explore the factors that will make the difference in how to respond and recover.

CHAPTER 7

INITIAL RESPONSE

Incidents and errors express themselves in infinite ways. The initial response requires us to think on our feet, diagnose and be ready to respond with flexibly to the uniqueness of each event.

Developing Response Flexibility

Here's a quick note on training people to respond to unexpected situations.

When we have the luxury of responding in slow time to anticipated issues (risky work situations, difficult conversations, strategic interactions), planning and the use of procedures or proven practices are great options. The higher risk the business activity (aviation, power generation and distribution, high rise construction, or health care), the more likely it will already be highly proceduralized. Generally, the more regulated the activity is, the more likely this will be so.

However, planning and routine procedures no longer fit when we need to respond to emergencies, or to unforeseen or unique events.

Even in less risky operations we often overemphasize procedural training in spite of the impossibility of foreseeing every possible eventuality. The attempt to create procedures for everything that could possibly happen is futile. Handcuffing organizations with procedures will limit behavioral flexibility to creatively find new solutions. Eventually they impede people's ability to achieve their goals.

To prepare people for unanticipated events, to think on their feet, the most effective way is to involve them in simulations that are run in real time and involve as much sensory reality as possible. The simulations must feel as real as you can make it. Aircraft simulators, reality simulations of combat, kidnapping or terror attacks, fire drills, business disaster scenarios or some variation of these all come to mind.

Stabilize and Protect

The first duty in an initial response is to stabilize the situation. Stop the bleeding - be that actual blood, financial bleeding, oils spills, vehicle defects or reputations.

Are the people and the facility safe and secure? Is the situation stable or still in flux?

To anticipate the variety of specific possible responses you may encounter is beyond the scope of this volume. But despite the brevity of this section and its inability to address the specifics of your organization's circumstance, do not underestimate its importance!

Stabilizing means isolating the damage so that the negative effect is not wider spread.

Preserve the Wreckage

Once a situation is stabilized and secure, we need to ensure access to reliable evidence which will preserve the integrity of our investigations and allow for the generation of appropriate recommendations. To "preserve the wreckage" we must ensure that none of the evidence is disturbed and the site is not "contaminated."

Not only does this apply to physical evidence, but critically to the people involved. Victims, witnesses, and second victims (those whose actions may have inadvertently contributed to others being victimized) need to be treated such that memory is preserved, negative effects minimized and recovery promoted. Such responses can include first aid, medical treatment, post-traumatic stress interventions, counseling or monitoring and supervision.

How we approach the individual as we investigate - the interview – becomes the central focus of the next critical phase of each incident response.

But before we step foot into the interview, an insight into human communication patterns is required.

CHAPTER 8

CRITICAL COMMUNICATION PATTERNS

Investigation interviews and team approaches to analysis and recommendation are all about human communication. This chapter explores aspects of communication that support those tasks.

The Limits of Conscious Capacity

To get an idea of the capacity difference between the conscious mind and the unconscious, imagine a house with a grain of sand on the roof. The grain of sand represents the conscious mind; the house represents the unconscious.

The conscious mind attends to what we focus on minute by minute, second by second. The number of things it can pay attention to at any given time is surprisingly limited - 7 plus or minus 2 things, and much less when we're under stress. (Miller, 1956)

The unconscious, on the other hand (or other mind), processes a seemingly infinitesimal number of operations simultaneously - learning and storage, attitudes and beliefs, and control of "automatic" behaviors like breathing and heart rate, blinking and a whole variety of non-verbal reactions.

The so called "Mind/Body" connection is such that a change in one (the mind) automatically (unconsciously) causes a change in the other (the body) and vice versa. An embarrassing thought makes us blush. This is not conscious. We don't decide to send more blood to the capillaries of our cheeks. We blush automatically (unconsciously). An anxious thought creates a change in our breathing and pulse. In the other direction, when we engage in an enjoyable activity, we begin to feel more relaxed. Our stress moderates.

The importance of this phenomenon is ENORMOUS! Internal shifts have corresponding observable changes in the body (external behavior).

In an investigation the ability to notice these shifts allows you to identify when you need to probe for more detail. And why would that be critical? Consider this...

Deletions, Distortions and Generalizations

Because of this capacity shortage in our conscious mind, we tend to delete, distort and generalize when we communicate. If I describe what I did on my weekend I will leave out many specific details, either as unimportant or so as to not bore my listener with minutia. This is fine in a casual conversation between friends but not so when relating critical information in an investigation.

And when we're under stress, the conscious mind capacity gets even further limited. Consider the interviewee who has witnessed or experienced a traumatic event. They may have been traumatized themselves. They may have witnessed the event under less than ideal circumstances. And they may be anxious about what the consequences of the investigation will be for themselves.

None of this puts them into a resourceful state.

<u>The Brain is Literal. The Unconscious does not Process Negation.</u>

The brain is literal. When we speak the brain's attention is directed towards whatever is suggested. Using a negation, such as "don't", won't deter the brain from following the literal suggestion. Here's an old example:

Right now, don't think about an elephant.

Most people report they immediately picture an elephant in their mind, despite the direction to "not" think about it. The only way the brain can process the information is to think about an elephant.

This phenomenon raises serious flags about the appropriateness of some of the images we inadvertently put into people's heads when we're clumsy with our language. Consider the parent who says, "Don't spill your milk." The parent shouldn't then be surprised when the child spills their milk a few seconds later. (More about the tone used to express that thought, shortly).

It is more useful to say, "Grip the glass firmly." Here, no negation is involved. The suggestion is more specific and reinforces the desired behavior.

In the workplace, a similar example would be, "Don't forget your safety equipment." Then, after an incident, how surprised we are when the worker says he or she "forgot" their safety equipment. Instead say, "Remember your safety equipment. Put it on." Always express yourself in the positive, while referencing specific desired behaviors.

The use of specific words to direct attention is surprisingly effective. Recently a contractor was re-shingling the roof of our house. As his crew worked, I was trimming the hedge and casually watching their progress. They worked with all the proper tools, lanyards, and fall arrest equipment. When they stopped for a break, I wandered over, thanked them for working safely, said what a difference it made to me and that they were doing a really professional job. When they returned to work, I overheard one of them say to another "Don't leave those bundle wrappers there, that's not very professional." Coincidence? Maybe. But the brain responds literally. We need to choose our words with care.

Say you go to your boss and ask, "Why didn't you support me on that proposal?" Of course, his or her attention is now directed to all the reasons why they didn't or shouldn't support you. That's not the direction of thinking you hoped for.

Instead ask, "What would have to happen for you to feel good about supporting this proposal?" That turns their attention in a completely different direction. Their answer gives you useful information which you can use to adjustment your proposal and gain their support.

Tonal Shifts

When we end a sentence, our tone can rise, fall, or remain flat. Each of these puts a different meaning to the sentence. "The floor is dirty," spoken with a rising tone at the end of the sentence will sound like a question. The same sentence with a flat tone will sound like a statement. While a falling tone, "Clean the floor." implies a command.

Back to our earlier example of "Don't spill your milk." If this is delivered with a falling tone, the child unconsciously associates it with commands like "Shut the door" or "Put your coat on." We are essentially giving a non-verbal command to spill their milk. The "don't" reference just doesn't compute unconsciously.

Looking and Pointing

Where we look and point or gesture towards something we direct attention towards that thing. When we look and point at individuals, we non-verbally ascribe what we are saying at the moment about them.

Here's the rule of thumb in this regard:

Make eye contact when the information you have to deliver is perceived as positive by the listener and when rapport is desired.

Avoid eye contact when the information is negative and decontamination (from negativity) is desired.

Consider this classic investigation faux pas, often spoken while looking at the person and even gesturing towards them:

"This is not about Blame."

Of course it's about blame! You raised the issue, directing their attention to blame, while you looked at them and gestured towards them. OMG!

Memory

When people access memories of things they've experienced, they re-enter the state they were in at the time of the original experience.

Traumatic experiences have the potential to re-traumatize. When this happens, resourceful states and accurate recall become impeded. Also, people may not recall unconscious acts.

Be cautious when asking for recall of traumatic events. We'll examine techniques to deal with this sensitive situation later on.

Breathing

The #1 indicator of permission and resourceful states is whether people are breathing high or low. By cultivating this awareness, you will even gain the ability to "read" aspects of culture in an organization.

When we breathe low in the belly our lungs get a full load of oxygen, our brains are fully oxygenated and we think and process optimally.

Low breathing indicates people are OK with what we're talking about (permission).

When people move to breathing high in the chest you'll notice a corresponding backwards movement of the head (at least a quarter of an inch or centimeter) often described as being "taken aback." Internally that person is no longer getting a full load of oxygen, not fully oxygenating the brain and no longer in a resourceful state. We have probably referenced content they do not give us permission to address. Or it's a negative comment on our ongoing relationship.

Imagine someone at the doctor receiving this news "I'm sorry to tell you but you have…" The head goes back, the breathing rises in the chest. They go out of a resourceful state and into shock. The doctor then proceeds to tell them how they can get well again but they don't hear a word of it. The next doctor visit works better when they bring a family member so the information can actually be heard.

When people go out of state like that, our goal is to nudge them back into deep breathing and a more resourceful state. This we do by matching their body movements nonverbally. Breathing at the same rate as the other person is a very powerful way to build rapport. But we don't want to match high breathing. Instead, by making small movements that match their rate of breathing, we can build rapport. Once we are in rapport with the other person, we can lead them by gradually slowing down our own breathing and talking slower until we're relaxed, and talking at the rate we would like them to breathe. People tend to entrain themselves to others with whom they have rapport.

Mirroring and Matching

Mirroring and matching allows us to build rapport, strengthen relationships and put others at ease. Mirror body postures and match other non-verbal communication such as tone, volume, speed, and facial expression.

Reflecting back the behavior of others is based on a deeply programmed evolutionary bias towards sameness. We unconsciously feel that people like us must be "OK" while those who are not like us can't be quite as OK as we are. Although this sounds racist or sexist, which it is if taken too far, generations of our ancestors survived because they could distinguish between themselves and dangerous creatures or other people from hostile groups. Survival depended on preferring sameness and being wary of difference.

In one well known set of police/suspect interview tapes in a high profile Canadian murder case that was posted online, the police interviewer had built such a level of rapport with the suspect that the suspect says, "You don't have to call me by my full name, call me this."

With rapport comes low breathing, better resource states, clearer memory and less resistance to opening up.

Two cautions here. First, avoid paraphrasing. When we change people's words they can begin to believe that we aren't hearing them. Too few words in English have synonyms that mean exactly the same. Whenever possible repeat their first choice words to gain rapport and demonstrate understanding.

Second, mirroring and matching does not require some form of slavish mimicry to the point where the other person feels they are being mocked. Be subtle. Match motion with motion (even if it's not exactly the same motion), and stillness with stillness. And once a good rapport is established, back off from the mirroring and matching.

Credibility and Approachability

Michael Grinder points out that non-verbals are associated with being either credible or approachable. Using each to specific purpose vastly increases your communication effectiveness.

Credible body language includes:
- sitting very still
- head straight on top of the shoulders
- head still and being silent when listening
- wrist straight, palms down
- weight evenly distributed
- using a flat tone ending down

Approachable body language includes:
- leaning forward
- head forward and tilted
- head bobbing and sounds like "uh huh" when listening
- wrist bent, palms up
- body slanted, weight more on one leg
- using a tone that goes up and down ending high

REMEMBER: To get people's attention and build rapport we have to meet them in their version of reality and on their preferred channel(s), no matter how bizarre their version of the world may seem to us. This allows the doors of influence and communication to open.

Resistance is a comment on us. Are we flexible enough to enter the other person's world and work out from there?

In summary:

- Conscious capacity limitations produce deletions, distortions and generalizations as a natural phenomenum of communication
- The brain is literal and the unconscious does not process negation
- Tonal shifts can change meaning
- Looking and pointing ascribes the topic to the listener(s)
- Traumatic memory can re-traumatize
- Breathing is the most important non-verbal to watch for
- Mirroring and matching builds rapport, and
- Credible and approachable non-verbals are different

Practice and master your communication skills. They'll serve you well beyond the interview situations that we'll examine next.

CHAPTER 9

THE INTERVIEW

<u>Data Gathering – NOT Analysis</u>

Since the interview is *the* pivotal encounter in our response to errors, this chapter offers a bouquet of techniques for your consideration.

But before we go there, there is a ***major caution*** that **must be acknowledged.**

<u>**The interview is for data gathering. It is not for analysis. It must be completely separated from any hint of analysis.**</u>

Here's the reason.

A cause-and-effect approach, y causes x, always generates the dreaded "Why?" question or its variants: "Why did you do that?" "What were you thinking?" "What's the reason?" Each presupposes that you must have done this deliberately, that you had a motive, a reason, a rationale.

This suggestion of blame, fault, or intention is totally devoid of reality once you accept the Law of Human Performance from Chapter 6, that well-intentioned people occasionally and unconsciously make honest errors when faced with conflicting goals and constrained resources, Yet asking "Why?" and implying blame is what happens all too often. Blaming, seeking fault, or questioning intention is a one-way ticket to having most interviewees clam up. This spreads the word that these events are indeed about fault despite managerial platitudes to the contrary.

As soon as you ask "Why?", or as soon as you ask, "What should you have done?" (the classic hindsight bias), you've entered analysis and interrogation, you seek the explanation, the reason, the motive.

Analysis *contaminates* data collection.

Just because your form or format includes data gathering, analysis and recommendations in one document does not mean you have to do so in one session.

When fault finding implies interrogation, there is no return to interviewing.

In our workshops we use Jenga blocks to illustrate this issue, based on the example by Todd Conklin and his colleagues. The Jenga blocks are stacked in alternating layers of three to create a tower. The objective is to remove a block during your turn and, as the pile gets more unstable, to avoid being the one whose turn causes the tower to fall. After viewing a video of a workplace incident, the group brainstorms all of the contributing factors and each person is assigned some of those factors. As they take turns removing the Jenga blocks, representing each of the contributing factors, the tower gets increasingly more unstable until it finally falls during the "loser's" turn.

Incidents in the complex reality of our workplace inevitably involve a multitude of contributing factors, many of which are what Conklin and others call *latent conditions* within the system. Each of these contribute to the instability of that system which, like the tower, eventually culminate in an error event, which will now be "blamed" on the person who removed the last block - the loser, the person who precipitated the event.

In Jenga everyone wins except the one loser who must take responsibility regardless of the actions of the other players or the design of the game.

When we focus on blame, when we fail to get the full picture from those involved, when the culture becomes error intolerant, we seldom get down to addressing the complete variety of latent conditions that contributed to an event - and which will inevitably lead to the next one.

REMEMBER: Our levels of error tolerance and the ways we respond to error events shape our safety culture.

So, on with our data gathering interview.

Imagine coming into an interview. You're nervous. Perhaps even upset. You face not just one, but a panel of people looking sternly your way. You have no idea what you'll be asked. You're not sure what the outcome will be, maybe punishment. And then you're told to relax.

No problem? There probably is.

Intimidating? Without doubt.

Feeling resourceful? Not a chance.

Yet this is often the experience of job candidates, victims and witnesses in investigations, children with upset parents, and direct reports with their bosses.

Clearly fraught with unintended clumsiness, such crucial encounters quickly set the stage for subsequent success or failure.

And we can do *much* better than that.

Investigation Interview Goals

All interviews have a common goal - to hear an interviewee's story and get a "read" on them. The general assumption about incident or error investigation interviews is that the purpose is simply to gather facts, witness accounts and opinions from the subject matter experts – the witnesses who experienced the event.

This crucial contact sets the tone for subsequent action and success. Beyond data gathering at least 4 other opportunities present themselves:

1. To help restore the full memories of the victim, witness or "second victim"
2. To preserve and restore the psychological health of the interviewee
3. To preserve and enhance the integrity of the interviewer
4. To contribute to the recovery of the organization

1. To help restore the full memories of the victim, witness or "second victim"

We want to restore the memories of the interviewees so as much detail as possible can be retrieved as accurately as possible. (Note: "second victims" are others involved in an incident who have been affected beyond the primary victim, such as someone who triggered an event that harmed someone else.)

Often people involved in incidents experience events under less than ideal circumstances and often while they themselves are in less than optimal states. And when those experiences are traumatic, the memories themselves may not only be painful but can also re-traumatize them. Plus unconscious (automatic) actions and behaviors may not be remembered at all.

Taking time to put the interviewee at ease, to control the interview environment, and to provide a preview of what's to come, all contribute to establishing rapport. The more comfortable the interviewee, the more likely memory retrieval will be accommodated.

2. To preserve and restore the psychological health of the interviewee

We need to pay attention to their psychological recovery. The interviewees may be "shaken" by the event(s) in question, worried about whether they will be punished in some way or blamed by others. They may even be suffering from ongoing effects of PTSD.

When they are comfortable enough to talk about their feelings and current state of mind, more possibilities open up to aid that recovery. This may take the form of referrals to an Employee Assistance Program or to treatment, recommendations for supervisory and/or peer monitoring, follow-up such as re-clarification of roles or training, and reassurance that blame is not on the table for honest reporting of facts.

3. To preserve and enhance the integrity of the interviewer

Incident investigations are often conducted by organizational leaders, either frontline supervisors, staff support departments like Safety or HR, or senior managers. The interviewer is quickly tainted when an interview includes accusations or even suggestions of blame, associations with punishment, or impressions that there is more interest in just "getting this thing over with" than listening to the interviewee's concerns.

Then stories spread. Others come to believe that as that person was treated, so will I be. This diminishes the interviewer's credibility and ability to be effective in the future.

4. To contribute to the recovery of the organization

Avoid seeing investigation as a dreaded administrative task to be done as quickly as possible. Think of it as an opportunity to examine how the organization is working, to fine tune, and to set future direction.

Think beyond the simple collection of facts and data. The interview is a unique intervention, a pause in normal operations that allows us to re-focus and to set direction for workers, leaders and the organization as a whole. It's like first contact in a sci-fi movie, the chance to get it right, right from the start.

Rapport

The more comfortable people are with both the person(s) interviewing them and with the interview environment, the easier they access resourceful states to aid memory, truth telling and recovery. As obvious as this seems it's often trickier in reality and requires deliberate practice and effort to master. Fortunately, we aren't restricted to investigation activities to practice rapport. Every encounter with others is an opportunity to observe, practice techniques and fine tune.

The fundamental tenet underlying rapport, as mentioned in the previous Chapter, is that people who are like you must be OK and people who aren't like you can't be quite as OK as you are.

And the most important technique" to achieve rapport, to be "like" the people you face, is to mirror and match.

As a rule of thumb, rapport is used when the other person is reasonably well behaved and when the information you have for them is perceived positively. When they behave poorly or they perceive information as negative, rapport is avoided. Avoid being associated with negativity which will damage relationships and maintain the other person in an unresourceful state.

What to mirror and match? Breathing, tone, volume, gestures, posture, movement or stillness, facial expressions, or language patterns. Helpful behaviors like leaning forward, head nods or words of encouragement are useful.

Repeat back the other's words rather than paraphrasing them. Using different words can sound like you're not listening accurately. When you want more information consider repeating their words exactly but turning your tone up at the end of the statement to turn it into a question. Questions based on their words are preferable and require less internal processing on their part.

Keep in mind that rapport is best learned experientially. Practice with others. Attend learning events. Every conversation is an opportunity to fine tune your skills.

Number of interviewers

Often in investigations, and certainly in job interviews, we find ourselves face to face with a panel or group of people. Since we're seeking to put an interviewee at ease, aid their memory processes, and encourage opening up, having them experience what looks more like an inquisition than a one-on-one conversation seems at cross purpose to our goals. That's not to say that there is no value in additional people being present but rapport with one person is challenging enough without the presence of others who may be less familiar faces to the interviewee. So how do we balance this?

First identify and introduce yourself. Then identify and introduce any others. Clarify what their roles may be during the interview, e.g. note taking or observation. If union representatives are present, clarify with them ahead of time what their role will be. Stress the importance of allowing the interviewer to proceed uninterrupted. Providing an outline of how the process will unfold and what the goals are can reassure the union representative that the best interests of their fellow member are being honored and that the interview is strictly for data gathering.

It's critical to have anyone other than the interviewer sit *behind* the interviewee, literally out of the interviewee's range of view, so that their presence does not interfere with the rapport process being developed between the interviewer and the interviewee.

This raises the issue of how note-taking should be done.

Note-taking

Imagine being interviewed in an investigation or for a job by an interviewer who spends most of the time with their head down making notes rather than conversing with you. What signal does that send about attention to rapport? To relationship building? It's impossible to feel rapport or get a sense that you're being listened to when you're confronted mostly with a view of the top of their head. And how could such an interviewer ever hope to notice the non-verbal shifts that signal changes of state and mark when additional questions should be asked?

So how do we maintain rapport *and* capture the information?

If you're the interviewer try saying this. "Please tell me your story in as much detail as you can so I can get a sense of what happened. No detail is too small so please be as detailed as possible. After that I'd like to go through it again so I can take some notes and ask questions to clarify. I'll probably need to ask you to slow down so I can keep up." Then listen with 100% attention to the interviewee.

If you have more than one person in the room, after seating them behind the interviewee, let them do the recording.

In either case remind the interviewee that this is t*heir* story and that any notes, once transcribed, will be provided to them for review to ensure that it accurately reflects what they have said. They get to approve the story.

To get note-taking exactly right, record the interview. It's remarkable that this is a common practice in many contexts but seldom used in the workplace. Yet what better way to ensure the accuracy of the record. This should appeal to both parties. In all likelihood recording will be reserved for more serious incidents. Once again the interviewee gets to review the transcript for accuracy.

The famous writer, personality and raconteur Studs Terkel would go into interviews with a tape recorder and then would "forget" to turn it on despite having gotten prior consent to use it. The interviewees would become concerned for him and remind him to turn it on. By accepting their help and acknowledging their permission, he promoted their continued cooperation throughout the interview. (Gray, 2011)

Just a thought.

Calibration

In addition to mirroring and matching another person, calibration is an important skill. Calibration entails watching for changes in the person's physiology as you interact with them. Paying attention to the details of posture, breathing, muscle tonus, or skin color allows you to monitor what's happening to them as they talk.

Changes signal opportunities to inquire further into the topic area being discussed when the changes occurred. "Tell me more about that." "Did I get that right?"

When we get completely involved in the content of what they are saying, often imagining it in our own mind, we can miss these subtle but important shifts in physiology. To allow yourself to focus on the person rather than just the content, use a recorder or ask one of the other interviewers, if there are some, to take notes on the content.

You can practice noticing these changes by watching others in conversations when you don't need to be involved in the content, or on TV with the sound off, or observing others at the mall or in a meeting. The more you practice, the more you'll be able to track both content and changes in physiology simultaneously.

Priming

You'll find this topic not only useful, but intuitively easy to master. There you've been primed.

Executive summaries in reports, overviews in presentations, pre-meeting agenda distributions or previews of what's to come in a conversation are everyday examples of priming. Why? First, we seem to make better sense of the information that follows when we get the overview at the beginning. Second, our willingness to put up with something that we don't like improves when we know what's coming, rather than having it sprung on us out of the blue and being surprised. Even if our willingness to accept something we don't like may not shift, at least our resistance will often moderate, albeit grudgingly.

Priming can also be used to set the tone for the interviewee. Use references like "easy", "relaxing" or "comfortable".

To prime an interviewee about the interview process. you can say something along these lines:

"Please tell me step by step, in as much detail as possible, all that you remember."

"We'll go through this twice, the first time I just want to get a clear picture in my head of what happened. The second time

I'll take some notes. Please be patient as I may ask you to stop occasionally so I can catch up."

"Once I've written up your account, you can correct it until you say it's right."

"I just want to understand your story. Once we've gathered all the information, an analysis will be done separately to figure out what prevention lessons can be learned. We sometimes need a follow-up session as well, to clarify information."

"Are you OK with the time right now? So we won't be interrupted, is there anything you need? Water? A washroom break?"

"So please relax, this will be as easy as remembering your phone number. What is your phone number by the way? There you go."

Summaries and reviews

Let the interviewee run with their story without interruption. When you make subsequent passes through the information, that's when specific questions or probes can be added. You've already primed them for this.

As you proceed, ask them to pause regularly and repeat back to them using as much of their language as you can. If you let them ramble on too long, it gets to be too much information to track.

Regular summaries and reviews not only improve clarity, they deepen the rapport.

You're expressing interest in clarifying their account rather than expressing your opinions or theories about what happened.

Turning statements into questions

In our training we include multiple opportunities for practice in calibration and rapport building. These can be applied to a variety of communication situations. Interviewers often struggle to come up with what we believe are the required or "best" questions to ask that unlock the nature of the question or issue in front of us. That's working too hard. Take your cues from the person you're talking to.

One of the easiest ways to do this is to repeat their words exactly and turn your tone up at the end of the sentence. The rising tone is heard as a question, as opposed to a falling tone which is heard as a command. "You've tried everything? And nothing ever works?" "And that's all there was to it?"

Using their words sounds natural to them. Questions that come out of the blue on the other hand require them to mentally examine the question, compare it to their own experience and then respond. They drop out of the story they've been telling. Their own words turned into a question keep them rolling along with more detail from the story without diversions to consider a question and whether or not it's relevant to the incident at hand. Standard questions on a form can be particularly problematic in this regard.

Naïve interviewers who read questions off of a form often experience resistance because the generic questions don't directly connect to the experience of the individual being interviewed. When those interviewers read off a series of causation factors and then ask which ones fit, interviewees face a dilemma. Do I force fit a cause to satisfy the form and the interviewer or just tell my story? What if my story is more complex than the listed factors account for?

By using their words with a rising tone you're simply asking them to fill in some of the blanks in their account.

Meta Model Questioning

We learned last chapter that it is normal for people to delete, distort and generalize. The field of NLP (Neuro-Linguistic Programming) offers a process to retrieve deleted or distorted information. You may want to pursue this in greater depth once you've mastered the technique of rising tone. The process is called the Meta Model.

There are patterns of missing information that can be retrieved. These patterns have names that may seem awkward at first but you'll notice that the examples, and the subsequent questions to retrieve missing information, are obvious.

Just as rapport building takes practice, so too does mastery of the Meta Model. As people talk, listen for missing information. Be curious. Notice which questions prompt the missing details.

Here are some examples and questions from Dr. Richard Gray's book *Interviewing and Counseling Skills: An NLP Perspective*. I highly recommend this readable book.

Deleted referential index
- Example - "The alarm was sounded, the door was opened, the error was missed…"
- What's missing – By whom?
- Questions – Who sounded the alarm? Who opened the door? Who missed the error?

Unspecified referential index
- Example - "That's the way it is, it was just there, something happened…"
- What's missing – What specifically is being referred to?
- Questions – What's "the way it is"? What was "just there" and how did it get there? What specifically "happened" and how do you know?"

Generalized referential index
- Example - "Supervisors don't care, they always brush me off, management doesn't understand…"
- What's missing – About what? In every case without exception? Always?
- Questions – They "don't care" about what? Always? Management doesn't understand what?

There are a number of these patterns but one more in particular is worth noting.

Nominalization

Nominalizations are action words (verbs) that have been transformed into nouns (things) or nominalized. They get treated like they are things and not actions. The test of whether something is a thing that exists in reality is the wheelbarrow test. Could I put this thing in a wheelbarrow, like a brick or a book or, presumably if my wheelbarrow was big enough, a car or a galaxy (which also used to be a car now that I think of it)?

When people nominalize an action they tend to feel like they've lost control. It's no longer something they're doing that they *can* control. It's something that is being done to them. (Perfect for sustained victimhood.)

So "I need love, but I'm stuck" (you can't put a pound of love in a wheelbarrow). Contrast that with "How can I be more loving in a way that's meaningful to another?"

And so it goes with nominalizations, like depression (which apparently "happened" to me versus how am I depressing myself or dwelling on depressing things). Other classic nominalizations include willpower, patience and of course "Safety."

Sorry, you can't put an ounce of safety in a wheelbarrow. "Our safety sucks around here." "We need more safety." "Safety is job 1." No, no, no! Safety is a set of risk-focused, behavioral and equipment standards (things) and a set of operational processes (actions) established to maintain clear and reasonable standards and to ensure (or at least maximize) their compliance. It is a process of acting, not a thing you can have or lose.

Nominalizing tends to remove us from the responsibility for self-initiation and personal action. Stick with the verbs! What do we do? What do I have to do?

During the interview you don't have to challenge every deletion, distortion or generalization. To do so would get tedious and erode rapport. You can always make notes on areas to come back to in subsequent interviews. As Dr. Gray states, "Good interviews happen in layers. They are an exercise in patience. They are thorough, but they do not need to be rushed." (Gray, 2011)

Cognitive Interviewing

Police interviewing has been influenced in the past by the well-known Reid Technique, a set of tools to assess a person's credibility and to get a perpetrator's confession. This technique uses eye contact, fidgeting and nervousness as indicators of deception. But polygrapher John Reid's interpretation of these behaviors is not supported by scientific studies (Gray, 2011). Furthermore, when officers cited these techniques as the means they used to detect deception, their ability to detect lies declined (Gray, 2011).

Fisher and Geiselman (1992) found that police interviewers interrupted a witness in less than 20 seconds on average, thereby impeding the memory process. And since the bulk of police interviewees are friendly witnesses, not perpetrators, a technique used for interrogation of suspects does not satisfy the four interview goals we previously established.

As an alternative Fisher and Geiselman offer the process of Cognitive Interviewing which they found elicited a median of 34% more recalled information. Not bad!

Cognitive Interviewing has 4 components:

- Report all details regardless of their apparent importance
- Change the sequence of recall
- Change the perspective
- Reinstate the context

Report all Details

- Tell me what happened with as much detail as comes to mind regardless of how important or not they may seem.

Notice that this reflects the open-ended approach that was discussed earlier. It lets the story be told without interruption or the use of leading or distracting questions.

Different Sequence or Order

- Tell me again from the end back to the beginning.

Witnesses may struggle to accomplish this backward storytelling but it generally yields additional information and confirms the sequence of events.

For those of you concerned about lying on the part of a witness, this technique can offer some clues. Most people will, despite the effort, be able to tell their own experience backwards. When someone however has made up a story often the cognitive overload created by trying to reverse a rehearsed story overwhelms their ability to tell it in the opposite direction. Also contrived stories tend to be repeated verbatim each time whereas remembered experience tends to vary when repeated as different details are recalled.

Different Perspectives

- Imagine you were a fly on the wall, or were in "x"s shoes, or saw this from the other side, what would that look like?

- If you were to observe this from a different distance, closer or farther away, or from above what would that be like?

Interviewees can be re-traumatized when they recall a disturbing event from a subjective perspective. When they retell the event, they relive it as if it were still happening.

These questions help them move to a safer perspective. By moving to an objective observation point in their mind's eye, they bypass the emotion pain of re-experiencing a traumatic event. Because they feel safer, they can often retrieve additional information.

Context

Let's not underestimate the importance of this line of questioning, again –

Context is King!

Context is the reason why people often do what they do. Context frames what is normal. It's the way we do things around here. Context or "culture" is a set of behaviors that a group has come to think of as "normal".

Remember the example of teenagers? Why do you want to go there? "Cause everyone's going there." Why are you doing that? "Cause everyone's doing it." What do you want one of those for? "Cause everyone has one."

And yet, incredibly, context is the thing that many investigation formats are silent on.

Because context is a broader consideration than the specific details of a remembered incident, questions about context can be more specific (without leading).

Context regarding what?

- Physical work environment
- Individual's state of mind, fitness, attention, feelings
- Social environment– group norms, worker/supervisor relations, worker/worker relations, organizational culture

- Context Questions
  - Tell me what you noticed (remember) about the physical environment (conditions) that day.
  - Tell me what your day was like that day. How were you feeling?
  - Tell me what it's like working in that group (on that team or in that department), for Supervisor X, or at that organization.

If you're curious enough to test out the effectiveness of Cognitive Interviewing, try it out with someone. Ask them to describe some incident that's happened to them recently. Ask the types of questions that you've been using in your existing investigation form or format. Then give it a second go using the Cognitive Interview components. You'll be pleasantly surprised by the amount of additional detail you get!

Clean Language

Clean Language is a process of interviewing developed by the late New Zealand counselor David Grove for therapeutic and coaching situations. Clean Language allows for questions that prompt the interviewee to provide more detail without the interviewer's language getting in the way or lapsing into leading questions.

Note in the format provided below that questions are structured around aspects of the details being sought – detail, location, time, or source. The format consists of a neutral question stem that is completed by adding the words that the interviewee has just stated, and, of course, ending with a rising tone.

Detail

And is there anything else about (witness words)?
And what kind of (witness words) is that (witness words)?

Location

And where is (witness words)?
And whereabouts (witness words)?

Time

And then what happened?
And what happened next?
And what happens just before (witness words)?

Source

And where could (witness words) come from?

The questioning is enhanced when the interviewer pays attention to the vocal qualities that they themselves are using and alternates between mirroring and matching the interviewee's patterns and their own.

- Witness-generated words, added into the question stem, should also match the way in which the witness speaks.
- Interviewer generated words, should be spoken s-l-o-w-e-r and with a consistent, rhythmic, and curious tone. (Lawley and Tompkins, 2000)

The Sheet of Glass Technique

Have you noticed how people tend to look up, down, or sideways when trying to remember something. Then they seem to "land on it" and bring forward the memory? This is the phenomenon known as eye accessing cues. In addition to our tendency to point and look at things that we're talking about, we use spatial cues (or where we look) to access certain memories and processing information.

Awareness of this tendency can help with interviews. As an interviewee speaks, notice that they will often gesture towards or point and look to places in space as they describe their experience. They are literally re-living the experience as if it were unfolding in front of them.

Imagine a sheet of glass between you and them. Pay attention to the picture they are painting in the space between you on that sheet. As you regularly summarize and review what you're hearing, point to the places in space as they did and notice if they concur with your descriptions. It is easier to imagine the image(s) than to only process the verbiage.

The more ways that we can enter their world, their reality, and their experience, the more we can understand, signal that we are listening and get the full picture.

Follow-up Interviews

As you recall we prime the interviewee that there may be follow-up interviews. "Good interviews happen in layers. They are exercise in patience. They are thorough, but they do not need to be rushed." (Gray 2011)

Use second or third interviews if the interviewee becomes upset or emotional, if you need to clarify or get more information, or if you need to identify other areas to pursue. Regarding the latter, you will want to identify if there are others who have some relationship to this event who should be interviewed, or if there are other contributing factors that need to be considered.

At this point you can also clarify what role, if any, the witness can expect to play in the analysis or the generation of recommendations.

<u>Some Notes on Mastering Techniques</u>

Since mastery of these techniques involves a lot of non-verbal communication skills, understanding them intellectually will only take you so far. Getting to Carnegie Hall as they say involves practice, practice, practice. You can work on many of these skills during any daily activity where it would be appropriate to do so.

And consider "chunking" the skill sets down. Practice one aspect at a time. Today I'll listen for people's tone. Tomorrow I'll watch how they gesture. Another day I'll practice priming, and so on.

<u>Who should Investigate?</u>

Many organizational investigations are conducted by a frontline supervisor. Generally, the greater the severity or impact (e.g. a breach of legal, professional or ethical standards) the more likely people further up the chain (managers, HR, Safety) or outside bodies (regulators, governing bodies) will be involved.

For most organizations the frontline supervisor is the natural choice. They know the work, they know the people, and they have a vested interest in the outcomes.

Keep in mind that for all investigators proper training is a must.

When choosing who to investigate, consider the relationship that person has, or will have with the interviewees. If past relationships have been negative and relationships are rocky, then gaining rapport and openness may be impossible. They may be "anchored" to negativity or expectations of punishment. Similarly, if the interviewer has to maintain relationships after the investigation and its outcome may be perceived as negative, subsequent working relationships may be difficult.

Bringing an interviewer from outside the immediate work area allows someone to come in without any baggage. However, bringing in outsiders tends to raise the perception of the significance of the event in the mind of the interviewee who may approach the investigation with increased caution.

Because of the unique nature of these factors, you may need to consider situational differences when determining who should investigate.

Ask yourself, who can best deliver on all of the goals of an effective interview? Who can make the interviewees feel even better on way out than they did on the way in?

Where to interview

"I'd like to see you in my office." Now that phrase can raise the hairs on the back of the neck. It does so when the boss's office is already associated with negativity. No "catching people doing things right" and putting that in their file around here!

If the office is negatively perceived, or if it is positively perceived and you want to keep it that way (free from contamination by a negatively perceived event) then seek out a neutral location to do the interviews. You may even consider going to another building if the contamination could embrace a larger chunk of the worksite than the office itself.

Final thoughts

The interview is a "make it or break it" moment. If your intention is to initiate recovery, heal, bring the operation back to stasis and improve performance and relationships, you have an obligation to get it right.

Someday when you're facing an interview of your own, say the one to get that big promotion, and you get asked the "What are your strengths?" question, I like to image your looking the interviewer straight in the eye and saying, "I do world class investigations and interviews. I'm trained in it. I'm good at it. And my department has continuously improved because of it."

Then let the world beat a path to your door!

CHAPTER 10

HOW NOT TO GET SHOT

Special mention must be made to "How Not to Get Shot".

While the "How Not to Get Shot" approach is not specific to interviews, the technique is both applicable and invaluable.

We've been taught for years to look people in the face, smile and nod. What if that only worked in some circumstances but was completely inappropriate in others?

Turns out that's exactly the case.

When folks are well behaved and the information you have for them is positively perceived by them, then looking them in the face, smiling and nodding is great for building rapport.

This does not work when people are poorly behaved or need to be confronted or when you have news for them that's disappointing in their eyes. Why? When people get upset, shocked or otherwise react negatively to bad news, they tend to breathe high in the chest and get less oxygen to the brain. If in that instance you stand in front of them, facing them, you risk being associated or "anchored" to the feelings they're experiencing. After a few repeat experiences like this or even one highly emotional one, just seeing you will re-rigger those same negative feelings, reducing your ability to maintain rapport or to influence positively.

Rather than send an interviewee into shock with some piece of information or request to access memory, our goal is to keep them breathing low and to help them to stay calm and resourceful.

Yet, in an interview situation, there may be a time when traumatic memories need to be accessed or when you have to confront an interviewee with evidence that contradicts their statement.

In *The Elusive Obvious – The Science of Non-verbal Communication* (2007), Michael Grinder offers a brilliant technique which he calls "How Not to Get Shot".

Remember those messengers of old who got a spear through them when they told the emperor that the battle had been lost? We neither want to be shot as the messenger of disappointing news nor to lose rapport during the course of an investigation interview.

"How Not to Get Shot" delivers on three goals: it allows the interviewer to deliver negatively viewed information, maintains the interviewee in a resourceful state, and preserves the relationship between the two parties. This technique is useful in a wide range of situations beyond interviewing. Please keep in mind that practice is critical to mastering any interpersonal skill.

It's also useful during difficult conversations to "prime" the interviewee by referring to the value of the inquiry despite its sensitivity. Consider saying something along these lines: "As hard as talking about these things may be, it will make a big difference to others who can learn to avoid a similar situation."

And if accessing traumatic memories starts to re-traumatize the interviewee, stop that line of questioning, pause, take a break and redirect their attention to another topic.

How Not to Get Shot

There are eight components to the technique.

1. Go Visual

One of our goals is to decontaminate ourselves from being tagged with negativity. Having the interviewee look at us while receiving bad news obviously is not preferred. So what's the option? Go visual. Represent the bad news on a piece of paper, a white board or even gesture towards your palm or some point in space. Have the listener's attention directed to some other location rather than looking solely at you.

But if I held up a piece of paper with the bad news on it but held it in front of me, I'd still be lined up with that negative message and still risk being "shot." So just going visual is not enough.

2. Off to the Side

When I hold the paper or bad news off to the side, at arm's length, now it is separated from me and provides a different location for the listener to direct their attention.

Yet even that may not be enough if I continue to make eye contact with the listener while holding a visual message off to the side.

3. Listeners follow your eyes

Try this. If you're on the sidewalk at some busy intersection one day, stop and stare curiously up into the sky. You'll be startled at how many people will be drawn to follow your gaze upwards to see what's there.

Listeners follow our eyes. If I put my visual message off to the side but maintain eye contact, they will continue to look at me.

Instead, move your hand and eyes simultaneously as you look towards and gesture to the visual message held at arm's length, then maintain your gaze looking at the bad news for whatever length of time you are referring to it.

4. Use the Third Person

While referring to the problem or negative news refer to it in the Third Person - *the* problem, *the* report, *the* contradictory evidence as opposed to *your* report or *your* evidence. References to *your* or *yours* are in the Second Person – avoid these in favor of the Third Person reference.

5. Separate the Problem from the Solution

The visual, off to the side, gestured toward and looked at, represents the problem, the issue. The person who we look at when referring to the solution, is the solution, the one who can clarify and provide additional insight. Separating the two non-verbally is the essence of decontaminating yourself from negative associations, of maintaining rapport (We're OK, the problem's over there), and of keeping the interviewee in a resourceful state rather than lapsing into shock or resistance.

6. Use Voice Patterns Systematically

Grinder elegantly articulates the importance of continuing the separation by adding the systematic use of voice patterns. His work identifies a flat tone ending down as associated with credibility and a rolling tone ending up as associated with approachability.

When referring to the issue or problem use the credible voice pattern. When referring to and looking at the person, use the approachable pattern.

7. Be Specific Rather than General

We already know that we tend to generalize, delete and distort. Lapsing into generalizations doesn't cut it when we're seeking clarity regarding the story that's being told.

8. 90 Degrees

You've probably noticed that eye-to-eye contact can convey aggression in some circumstances. Think about the boxers' stare down at the weigh in or a predator/prey situation in the wild. When you converse directly opposite the interviewee, it makes it more difficult to direct attention away from yourself, off to the side. And the interviewee is always facing you regardless if you're discussing the person (the solution) or the issue.

Positioning yourself at 90 degrees, say across the corner of a table, helps facilitate "Not Getting Shot".

Again, the more you practice, the more "How Not to Get Shot" will become a natural part of your repertoire.

For more detail, resources and video support, consider referencing Grinder's original work, *The Elusive Obvious – The Science of Non-verbal Communication* (2007).

CHAPTER 11

ANALYSIS

Once we have gathered data through interviews and the collection of physical evidence, we're ready to begin analysis.

In Chapter 4 we pointed out the importance of having the right people in the room. The same is true of Analysis. "More heads are better than one."

As we move to re-frame our error response from one of interrogation, blame and correction to one of interview, understanding and organizational development, use the term "Learning Teams" as opposed to "investigators" to set a more positive and appropriate tone.

Learning Teams

Todd Conklin describes his organization's Learning Team strategy in his wonderful *Pre-Accident Investigations* (2012). He further describes the process in *Better Questions – An Applied Approach to Operational Learning* (2016). Both are highly recommended.

Learning Teams are ad hoc, informal groups formed to explore the organizational learnings which can be gleaned from an incident or near miss. Rather than ceding the sole responsibility for this to a supervisor, the Learning Team is a group of leaders, workers, and subject matter experts pulled together by a manager at any level. The impetus to do so is any error incident or issue which requires more attention.

That's not to say that every incident can or will be subject to a Learning Team analysis. Resource constrained organizations will always make cost/benefit decisions when deploying those constrained resources and may need to be selective when engaging Learning Teams. As organizational learnings continue to amass and resources allow, the application of Learning Teams can be broadened to more and more events and issues.

How do you implement?

Like any intervention, the starting point is buy-in from senior leadership. A move from "crime and punishment" to "diagnosis and treatment" requires a challenge to the status quo. Hopefully this book provides the ammunition you need for just that.

To promote the move to Learning Teams, create a presentation that reviews the hazards of traditional investigation including an honest assessment of how successfully your current system has been producing both the system changes and the performance changes you want. Consider referencing works by the likes of Sydney Dekker or Todd Conklin to demonstrate the state of the art that's being used successfully in high reliability industries such as aviation or power generation and distribution.

Bob Edwards offers the following benefits to the Learning Team approach (Edwards, 2015):

- Changes our discussion and response to failure
- Improves our understanding of errors & defenses
- Increases employee engagement
- Improves relationships with managers & employees
- Gives us deeper operational intelligence
- Helps us build better system & process defenses

- Moves us towards higher reliability
- Builds a new culture....

Selecting a group that has a good chance of success as a pilot site is recommended. Our models of whole system change are often not as robust as we would like. Attempts to change whole systems are often clumsy and only partially successful.

Pilot programs allow for revision and fine-tuning. They also create a "buzz." As one department starts to experience positive change, others start asking for it too. Success breeds success. And a successful pilot that can be rolled out to other departments is much more manageable than a complete system change.

Training will be required to understand this approach and to develop the necessary communication and analytical skills.

How do they work?

Get the right people together within one to three days after the initial interviews and data collection have been completed.

The group, as with most problem-solving teams, should number five to seven people. Consider including a knowledgeable coach, the area leader, the person involved, co-worker(s), staff or outside subject matter experts, safety reps and even neutral parties from other areas of the operation.

The format is:

- First session – Learning mode only
- "Soak time"
- Second session – analysis and recommendations

During the first session (an hour or so) review the data, compare to other known events, visit the site if appropriate, use visual representations (flip charts, white boards) and encourage input from all.

Soak time, time to reflect (a day or two), allows members to process the information, ask questions and do additional data gathering.

The second session may include an additional member for objectivity or additional perspectives. Evaluate existing defenses and consider where improvements are possible. Then develop recommendations.

As in any group problem-solving situation, a variety of analytical and creative solution generation tools can be employed. Consider Kurt Lewin's Force Field Analysis, Kepner-Tregoe's Analytic Problem Solving, Fault Tree Analysis, brainstorming and others. Some specific suggestions follow.

The Question of Questions

You'll note that while collecting data during the interview we opt for the most part to let the interviewee tell their story without interruption. Questions are asked on a second round for clarification and are triggered by the interviewee's testimony and their non-verbal behaviors. They also include Clean Language questions that do not lead or influence the interviewee's answers.

Analysis too invokes a series of questions to figure out what's going on or what happened. Every profession, trade or job function tends to have its own set of these whether it's the physician diagnosing, the electrician finding a fault or the operator locating a problem. Investigation and problem-solving formats have their preferred set of questions that, as we've noted, often reflect a bias towards one causation model or another.

But should we create an exhaustive list of 600 questions so that no contributing factors are missed? Or just leave a blank page? If we specify the questions, do investigators stop at the end of the list and ignore any others simply because they're not on the form? Do too many questions become unnecessarily complex? Does a blank page miss the opportunity to prompt the investigator to consider factors they might have missed?

To keep it simple and manageable, consider the "What's the Issue?" process (Chapter 2) and other formats to figure out what happened.

<u>What's the Issue?</u>

1. What's the **standard**?

   - What's a good job, well done? In terms of Safety? Quantity? Quality? Timeliness? Completeness?
   - What's acceptable versus unacceptable behavior?

2. Is the standard **reasonable**? Is it clear?

3. Who's **responsible** to carry out the standard? Is that clear?

4. **Can they do it?**

   - Is it a **competence** issue?
   - Do they have the skills and knowledge?
   - Is it an abilities issue?

5. **Do they do it?**

   - Is it a **compliance** issue? What's the frequency of non- compliance?
   - Do you have reliable evidence?
   - Would knowing why they don't do it give you useful information?

6. Are the necessary **resources** available?

- Time? Materials? Equipment? Authority? Budget? Info?

<u>Other Analysis Tools</u>

TOR Analysis

D.A. Weaver's TOR analysis (Technique of Operational Review) is an excellent tool to encourage non-judgemental discussion in a group setting. Group discussion buzzes and soars without any reference to blame. TOR is an analytical problem-solving tool involving a series of linked yes-no questions used in conjunction with a worksheet. See *The Art of Safety* (Phillips, 2008).

Additional Questions

The following list, gleaned from a variety of problem-solving and investigation sources, offers other useful questions for system inquiries beyond the presenting incident:

- What could have happened?
- Is there a trend? Is it improving or worsening?
- What's the difference between what happened and what could have happened?
- What changed regarding each difference?
- If our conclusions about the factors involved are correct, do they explain the event(s)?
- What factors led up to this event?
- What worked well? What failed?
- What's behind the factors that have been identified?
- Beyond the current fix, where else could this problem happen?
- Do other similar situations require attention?

Risk assessment

Risk assessment as a topic can and does fill many volumes on its own. But since it's not the principle focus of this book, you're encouraged to seek out more insight elsewhere. There are, however, some immediate practical strategies you can employ.

Risk assessment is not widely understood and often accepted at face value. In everyday conversations and in the media you may have noticed a tendency towards overgeneralization and risk perceptions confused with risk assessment. Think about the folks who won't fly yet believe that driving is safer. For more about risk calculation, consider reading *Thinking Fast and Slow* by Daniel Kahneman (2011) or *The Feeling of Risk* by Paul Slovic (2010).

Many investigation formats include a nod towards the chance of recurrence by assessing the severity and frequency. Often these include something along the line of "Is the Loss Severity Potential - Major, Serious or Minor?" and "Is the Probable Frequency Rate - Frequent, Occasional or Rare?" with attendant check-off boxes. Occasionally these will have a corresponding key to tell the investigator what those terms mean. More often than not there is no such key.

If nothing else, define those severity and frequency terms so that those completing your forms know what they mean and to get some consistency in applying them across the organization.

All risk assessments include three elements – the Risk or Odds that something will happen, the Potential Consequences of an incident and the Exposure to those risks. In the calculation of the Risks or Odds, risk perception rears its ugly head and interferes with more considered calculations. Try comparing the number of exposures to the potential hazard against the number of times that incidents or near misses have actually occurred rather than vague assertions of perceptual risk.

Risk assessment can get complex. Some approaches like system safety calculations, such as NASA would use, may be overkill for many workplaces.

For some quick and practical risk calculations, refer to *The Art of Safety* (Phillips, 2008). Go to http://www.artofsafety.ca/resources/ for reproducible copies of the Risk Calculator and the Risk Profile.

Incident Report Analysis

Another approach from *The Art of Safety* is "Incident Report Analysis", a single-page analysis of existing incident reports. This is a useful tool for identifying where changes are needed within the investigation reporting system and for attaching numerical ratings such that improvements can be measured over time. And it's easy to install. Go to http://www.artofsafety.ca/resources/ for reproducible copies of the Incident Report.

The Incident Report asks the manager (to whom the report writer or investigator directly reports) to evaluate seven aspects of report completion. Wherever the manager cannot assign full marks to a factor, he or she is asked to provide comments on what they want instead. As this gets fed back to the report writer, a continuous learning loop is established. Total average scores can be used over time to set targets for initial submissions of reports and to track and measure performance improvement.

Going Visual

As you think back to the previous thoughts on brain function in Chapter 8, "Critical Communication Patterns", remember that our conscious processing capacity is limited. Information that is processed verbally or "in our head" can quickly overwhelm the conscious mind. We compensate for this by going visual.

Try this simple ABC experiment. Off the top of your head how many two-letter combinations of A and B are there without repeating any letters? If you got 2 combinations, AB and BA, congratulations you're correct. Now, again off the top of your head how many three-letter combinations of AB and C are there? Fewer people can name the 6 – ABC, ACB, BAC, BCA, CAB, CBA. Finally how many four-letter combinations are there in ABC and D? Practically no one can name the 24 combinations off the top of their head. Yet if you start writing them down, your brain sees the patterns and fills in the rest. Test it out.

Even with only three variables no more complex than A, B and C we're already challenged when pressed to name the six combinations. Yet going visual allows us to see the patterns and the options.

Every incident investigation will likely involve a myriad of variables and details. Tying to juggle these and the relationships between them becomes impossible to do simply through discussion. Often when people attempt to solve problems or make decisions off the top of their heads, they either end up in indecision or "jump to conclusions" seeking a simple way out of the dilemma.

Go visual! Use Flip Charts, white boards, sticky notes, mind maps, whatever visual resources are available to the group. Get all the variables represented visually. Connect ideas to show relatedness. Not only will this tend to draw the group together on a jointly created product but it will also overcome the conscious processing issue by making all pertinent information available for examination during discussions. Projected images of information tend not to work as well because information disappears when we move to the next slide - out of sight, out of mind.

Go visual, go visual, go visual! You'll be glad you did!

The Great Detectives

Finally let's give a nod to the analytical skills of those fictional detectives whose exploits and ability to figure things out have intrigued us for decades. Arthur Conan Doyle's Sherlock Holmes, Agatha Christie's Hercule Poirot and Louise Penny's Inspector Gamache provide valuable insight into problem solving of any kind.

These investigators employed keen observation skills and similar, analytic approaches. You too can use their approaches to figure things out and to develop your own sensory acuity.

The great detectives regularly wondered:

- What's missing?
- What's not being said?
- What's different here?

These classic three questions are useful for investigating incidents. Asking "What's missing?" or "What's not being said?" prompts us to consider what else we want to know. "What's different here?" prompts us to examine how this situation is different from the standard or expectation. What aspects define that difference? What do you see, hear, or sense that makes you curious?

REMEMBER: Questions are your tools. Effective tool users practice to hone the design of their tools and the purpose for which those tools are best used.

CHAPTER 12

RECOMMENDATIONS AND IMPLEMENTATION

The final piece of the investigation is to translate the learnings from the analysis into recommendations.

Once again, our tools are questions which help us figure out what's happening.

<u>Is this a system issue or an individual performance issue?</u>

The "What's the Issue?" questions in Chapter 2 point to immediate focus areas. Questions 1 to 3, regarding standards and responsibility, focus on system requirements at the leadership level. Question 4, regarding skills, knowledge, and abilities, focuses on individual competency. Question 5, regarding compliance and non-compliance, focuses on individual variance or supervisory effectiveness (depending on frequency). Question 6 focuses on available resources and the possible need to revisit standards for reasonableness.

REMEMBER: One person's error does not imply everyone needs training unless a practical competence check confirms the problem is wide spread.

If it's a system issue, how large is the scope of the issue?

Is this at a crew or department level? A division or section? One location? The entire organization?

To what degree is interdepartmental, inter-locational or inter-level function an issue?

Does an intervention need to be directed at the level immediately above the areas that require better integration, cooperation, or communication? Apply "What's the Issue?" again at that level.

Recommendation Analysis

Test the quality and reasonableness of your recommendations by using these Recommendation Analysis questions:

1. Does the recommendation promote the psychological health, growth, ownership and resilience of the individual and the group? More independence or more dependency? More simplicity or more complexity? More productivity or more bureaucracy? Faster or slower response time? Better quality or less quality?
2. Has a Cost Analysis or a Cost/Benefit Analysis determined the best option?
3. What resources will be required to implement and follow-up until the recommended changes are established? Will these be available when needed?
4. Is acceptance of the recommendations by those who are affected by them critical to effective implementation? What are the implications of that?
5. Do those affected share the goals of the organization in implementing the change? What impact will the recommendations have on the team, the department or the people?

6. Could the recommendations interfere with the organization's ability to deliver its goals, services or products?
7. Do the answers to any of the above justify a revision of the recommendations?

Follow-up

If our recommendations pass the Recommendation Analysis, you'd think the next step would be straightforward - just do it. However, that is often not the case. Having reviewed numerous investigation records over the years, I'm surprised by the number of report files that make no mention of the follow-up. Were the recommendations carried out and completed? Was the situation monitored over time? Is there evidence that the follow-up was done? Maybe follow-ups were done but just not recorded. That, however, is problematic too.

Records are required to document that good faith efforts were made to remedy the situation and promote prevention. These records need to include an indication of the results over time. The best place to file this follow-up would be with the incident report and its recommendations.

Questions 3 to 6 of our Recommendation Analysis are critical!

Question 3 looks at the availability of needed resources. If, for instance, new standards imply a behavior change on the part of performers, will the supervisor have the time to do site visits or offer the coaching or training that may be required to install the new behaviors?

Question 4 asks if the recommendations are accepted by those who are affected by them. Buy-in by the group may be important. Could they sabotage the change effort because they disagree? How do we foster their involvement? What group interventions might be needed?

Question 5 asks if those affected share the organization's goals in implementing the change. If the individuals affected by the recommendations simply do not share the same goals as the organization, is the recommendation feasible? Is an arbitrary move without group involvement required? How must that differ from other approaches?

Question 6 examines a possible conflict between the recommendations and the organization's ability to deliver its goals, services or products. Chapter 6 offered the "Law of Human Performance." People who face competing organizational goals risk incurring errors. What if our recommendations solve one problem but make it harder to reach productivity goals? Will recommendations slow down processes or complicate systems? Will the trade-offs be acceptable? Or does some other solution need to be generated?

Recommendation Analysis is an *essential* step. When you envision the recommended follow-up and critically examine the impact of those recommendations, you'll immediately up the chances of success.

REMEMBER: Seemingly simple investigations are critical interventions into the systems of our increasingly complex workplaces. If we do this part well, the follow-up will fall into place. Give recommendations the attention and care they deserve and you'll be well rewarded.

CHAPTER 13

ACCOUNTABILITY AND FORGIVENESS

The Asoh Defense

Let's revisit Jerry Harvey (The Abilene Paradox) for another insight – The Asoh Defence.

When organizations pursue "0" injuries or errors as a goal or a "zero-defects" policy, it becomes more difficult for performers to own up to mistakes and expect to have them forgiven. "We have designed organizations that reduce risk taking, encourage lying, foment distrust and, as a consequence, decrease productivity." Mistakes hang like the sword of Damacles over the HR file, never to be expunged.

Harvey further comments "Show me a manager, subordinate, teacher, preacher, student, parent, child, politician, or anyone else who hasn't made a mistake in a year or two and I'll show you someone who has been afraid to try anything of significance."

On November 22, 1968 Japan Airlines Flight 2 approached San Francisco International Airport under the command of Captain Kohei Asoh. A former flight instructor with the Japanese military, he had over 10,000 hours flying commercial aircraft including over 1,000 hours on the DC-8 aircraft he was flying. With 96 passengers and 11 crew, he landed the plane two and a half mile out in San Francisco Bay in almost perfect alignment with the runway.

The landing was so gentle many passengers were unaware they were in the water until they looked out and saw sailboats going by. No one was injured, they barely got their feet wet being evacuated to shore, and the plane suffered minimum damage and was later rehabbed and put back into service.

Preparing for the National Transportation Safety Board hearings, lawyers and reporters settled in for the inevitable lengthy proceeding to determine cause, fault and blame.

As the throng of angry passengers, pilot and airline representatives, lawyers, reporters, and officials looked on, Captain Asoh was the first witness called. The first question asked was how he had managed to land two and a half miles out in the Bay in perfect alignment with the runway.

Now over the years, Captain Asoh's answer may well have become apocryphal, as much legend as truth, but it has had the sustaining power to persist.

Asoh's answer? "As you Americans say, Asoh f**k up."

With that, little of consequence could be added other than the clarification of details.

After a brief period out of the pilot's seat, Captain Asoh returned to the air and flew until his retirement. In Jerry Harvey's retelling of the captain's story, he popularized the phrase "The Asoh Defence".

Asoh boldly took responsibility for his own actions without blaming or taking responsibility for others.

Managers, teachers, and parents often assume responsibility for the actions of their direct reports, students, or children. Organizations perpetuate this by rewarding those in charge for the success of their people and punishing them when their folks don't deliver the results. This only reinforces the false belief that all accidents or errors are preventable and that we are in complete control of everything, including the thoughts and actions of others. There has to be a presumption that you are in complete control of others to justify our holding you accountable. And of course when one is at fault or to blame there can be no forgiveness, there must be accountability, there must be a consequence.

Since the consequences can be career threatening and follow us in our performance file forever, why would it be surprising that the result is to "reduce risk taking, encourage lying, foment distrust and, as a consequence, decrease productivity." And so the cycle rolls on - unless a rebalancing of accountability and forgiveness is addressed.

There is also a commonly held assumption that not all errors are forgivable, that severity changes error tolerance. They're inversely related. The greater the severity of the event, the less tolerance, the less forgiveness, and the more punishment must be applied.

The greater the severity of the outcome, the less likely that error tolerance will prevail over consequences.

Regulators deal with legal compliance. They have neither the same opportunities nor the same motivators to pursue the kinds of organizational recovery nor the forgiveness that we've discussed. Yet the law does allow for some error tolerance. In the case of homicide, distinctions are made between first degree murder, second degree and manslaughter. Similarly, compliance officers in health and safety administrations and departments of labor often apply discretion when considering whether to charge or not, based on contextual circumstances and intentionality.

But catastrophes, deaths, and critical injuries do not generally receive a "forgive and forget" response. Often family members, unions, shareholders, and society at large expect appropriate consequences to act as deterrents and to provide pathways to closure.

Organizations are pressured to respond in kind to regulatory sanctions (although kindness may not be the appropriate reference). What would be the optics if we don't mete out consequences? What does it say about how seriously we take these types of events? What are the consequences for senior executives if they don't to act?

When serious "sh*t" happens and regulators start meting out consequences, the organization will be expected to do the same despite the intentionality or non-intentionality of the actors in the event.

So not all errors are forgivable. The choice of where to draw the line between forgivable errors and consequence lies along a continuum that measures the severity of outcomes. The tipping point is drawn somewhere close to the catastrophic, fatal, and critical injury end.

But think back to the example of Martin Bromiley's "Just a Routine Operation" video. Near the end of the video Bromley explains that the people involved in his wife's incident had all returned back to work. And that was exactly what he wanted to happen. In this way those people could spread their personal learnings to their colleagues and be better clinicians themselves.

Bromiley, like most who lose a loved one, do not necessarily wish ill or retribution on those involved. Retribution obviously cannot bring back their loved one. What they do want to know is that the system was investigated, analyzed and that it responded professionally (Part 2 of this book) and that ongoing performance is more reliable and presents less risk (Part 1) as a result.

Forgiveness and reconciliation require evidence that the error producing factors in a system have been altered to reduce future recurrence.

If your organization cannot forgive, for whatever reason, it will still benefit when the line between forgiveness or no forgiveness is clearly identified and that performers know where that line lies. Workers may or may not agree with the choice of where the distinctions are drawn between honest error and the unforgivable but, when the standard is clear, at least the temperature of the reactions tend to go down.

It is also essential to be clear that the bulk of non-catastrophic events are forgivable opportunities to learn and fine tune our system.

REMEMBER: Consequences work as deterrents when acts are intentional, not so when acts are unintended:

It's impossible to punish your way out of error.

To explore this thorny choice further, consider these additional questions from Bob Edwards and Todd Conklin:

1. Was the learning event done **before** the discipline?
2. Would discipline normally be issued (based on this behavior) even if there was not an incident?
3. Did the work activity bypass a normal safety procedure (without an approved work-around document)?
4. Was the situation complex, requiring adaptation?
5. Is the proposed discipline consistent with past practice? Is past practice now appropriate?
6. Was the action a willful, intentional violation?

Of course, we play the "blame game" at home as well. Balancing accountability and forgiveness is tough for parents faced with inappropriate behaviors from their children, increasing so as they age. Ethics, morality, relationships, belief systems, and concern for future development and learning, all force us to stop and challenge our immediate gut reactions. The more parenting experience, the more opportunities we get to figure out how to balance that difficult middle ground. Yet as our children move into adulthood and move out, we no longer have any more authority or capacity to punish or direct them than we do to control all of the actions, motivations and thinking of our direct reports at work. We move more towards the tolerance, forgiveness and respectful influence that we would reserve for friends and other adults.

Our personal and family relationships can get complex and difficult. So too the workplace presents its own complexities - legal issues, cultural considerations, formal rules and regulations, hierarchical structures and a variety of authority levels. Getting the right balance of forgiveness and consequence in either arena is a unique challenge.

<u>Separate Investigation from Consequence</u>

If consequences do apply, remember to totally remove their application from the investigation activity. Avoid tainting the leadership or even "anchoring" physical locations like the supervisor's office to negativity by using the "How Not to Get Shot" technique. Consider removing such consequence assigning encounters from the locations where the worker has to return to work. Your intention here is to salvage relationships and keep the worker in a resourceful state.

At home consider the "time out" chair for younger children while keeping the rest of the house un-attached to any echoes of punishment. Sending someone to their room as a consequence and thus associating the room they will live in for years with punishment, is a questionable strategy at best.

It would be a wonderful world indeed if we could say, here is what works all the time, in all situations, to specifically balance accountability and forgiveness. Unfortunately, the complexity of human relations offers no simple answers.

Finding the appropriate balance will be your unique journey.

EPILOGUE

The Accountability/Forgiveness continuum is indeed a thorny concept to navigate, and so too is its cousin - Risk Tolerance.

When we avoid admitting our mistakes because of the repercussions they might bring, how much can we be learning either personally or organizationally? Culturally we tend not to either tolerate mistakes or reward risk-taking (unless it works out). Instead most organizations focus on and reward outcomes. It's a challenging task is to reward risk-taking and outcomes at the same time, especially if the outcomes were not what we had hoped for. But many high reliability organizations, such as nuclear power generation or aviation, do just that. They clearly commit to making risk tolerance and learning organizations work.

We can do the right thing, the right process, and still get the wrong outcome due to chance or luck. Conversely, we can do the wrong thing or use the wrong process and get a favorable outcome. Again, we get lucky. It's not the outcome that defines an error or mistake. It's the process. And it's the controllable aspects of our processes, and our behaviours in response to error that we must fine tune.

**Success is using a high-quality process, regardless of outcome.
Mistakes are using a low-quality process,
regardless of outcome.**
Steven Robbins (Newsletter –www.steverrobbins.com)

Is forgiveness a "high quality process", one to be applied when people step up and take the initiative to address non-routine or emergency situations? Does that forgiveness pre-empt punishment regardless of whether or not the outcomes are viewed retrospectively as positive or negative?

Sh*t will happen and errors will occur. That's normal. The real risk is to fall into the Blame Frame and miss the opportunity to promote the kind of organization and people growth that a more thoughtful response will generate.

It's hard to imagine an organization that can achieve continuous learning without careful consideration of risk-taking and the promotion of an error-tolerant culture.

Let's reward admission of error with forgiveness and with thoughtful investigation. If anything should be a target for accountability make it non-admission of error .

So there it is. Hopefully you've seen the merits of the reliability building and error response approaches that this volume offers. But let's face it. Swimming against the current to install new approaches is daunting, sometimes even, as mentioned, career threatening.

My experience in organizational development has left me with the impression that our models for wide-scale organizational change are imperfect and that our change efforts are often handled clumsily. I've seen more successful change arise from within the ranks of operations, independent of any formal process, because someone, some individual or group of individuals, simply took their ideas and started acting differently. And often they gained momentum from testing new approaches in pilot programs with groups that had a good chance of building success. Success spreads its own reputation.

At some time we all ask ourselves how we'd like to be remembered professionally, what we want to accomplish. Although it would be nice to see a grand vision installed, a great project completed or a magnificent accomplishment acknowledged, I'm not sure that's how it works.

In *Good to Great* (HarperCollins, 2001, page 14) Jim Collins put it this way:

> "Those who launch revolutions, dramatic change programs, and wrenching restructurings will almost certainly fail to make the leap from good to great. No matter how dramatic the end result, the good-to-great transformations never happened in one fell swoop. There was no single defining moment, no grand program, no one killer innovation, no solitary lucky break, no miracle moment. Rather, the process resembled relentlessly pushing a giant heavy flywheel in one direction, turn upon turn, building momentum until a point of breakthrough, and beyond."

It's not enough to just understand intellectually, you have to do it, apply the skills, practice the behaviors – relentlessly. Since culture is nothing more than a set of behaviors that a specific group has come to think of as "normal", the path to an improved culture is to start by setting new standards of what appropriate versus inappropriate behaviors are, and then committing to deliver on them daily.

Oh yes, you'll get it, you'll lose it, you'll get it back again, but eventually the new behaviors and the new ways to see the world around you will become normal too. And the flywheel will move.

The perseverance and resilience to simply apply your new skill sets and techniques on a regular basis, to influence one person, one group, one incident at a time - these are the keys to progress, to effective change, to being remembered.

TS Eliot said, "We shall not cease from exploration and the end of our exploring will be to arrive where we started and know the place for the first time."

We started this exploration with a nod towards the "secret of life" that flows from maintaining resourceful states and a sense of humor. Hopefully this volume provides the resources to define a starting point for you.

The rest is in your hands.
All the best.

READING AND VIEWING

Blackwell, Tom (January 16, 2015). Inside Canada's secret world of medical error: 'There is a lot of lying, there's a lot of cover-up', *National Post.*

Bourrier, Mathilde (1998). Elements for Designing a Self-Correcting Organization: Examples form Nuclear Power Plants, *Safety Management - The Challenge of Change* (Hale & Baram). England: Emerald Group Publishing.

Bromiley, Martin. Just a Routine Operation, https://www.youtube.com/watch?v=JzlvgtPIof4&t=7s

Collins, Jim (2001). *Good to Great.* New York: HarperCollins.

Conklin, Todd (2012). *Pre-Accident Investigations.* Ashgate Publishing.

Conklin, Todd (2016). *Better Questions – An Applied Approach to Operational Learning.* CRC Press - Taylor and Francis.

Crandall, Klein, and Hoffman (2006). *Working Minds – A Practitioner's Guide to Cognitive Task Analysis.* Cambridge: Massachusetts Institute of Technology.

Dekker, Sydney (2006). *The Field Guide to Understanding Risk.* Boca Raton: CRS Press.

Difford, Paul (2011). *Redressing the Balance: a Commonsense Approach to Causation.* South West England: Accidental Books Ltd.

Edwards, Bob (2015). Conference Notes – Enform Conference. Alberta.

Eliot, T.S. (1942). Little Gidding, *Four Quartets.* Faber and Faber.

Fault Tree Analysis Software, https://www.fault-tree-analysis-software.com

Fisher, Ronald P and R. E. Geiselman (1992). *Memory-enhancing techniques for investigative interviewing: The cognitive interview.* Springfield: Charles C Thomas.

Gray, Richard (2011). *Interviewing and Counseling Skills: An NLP Perspective.* Lulu.

Grinder, Michael (2007). *The Elusive Obvious – The Science of Non-verbal Communication.* Michael Grinder & Associates, www.michaelgrinder.com

Harvey, Jerry B. (1988). *The Abilene Paradox and Other Meditations on Management.* Lexington Books.

Kahneman, Daniel (2011). *Thinking Fast and Slow.* New York: Farrar, Straus and Giroux.

Kepner-Tregoe's Analytic Problem Solving Workshop

Kirkpatrick, Donald. Four Levels of Training Evaluation, https://www.kirkpatrickpartners.com

Kirkpatrick, James D. and Wendy Kayser Kirkpatrick (2016). *Kirkpatrick's Four Levels of Training Evaluation.* Alexandria: ATD Press.

Lawley, James and Penny Tompkins (2000). *Metaphors in Mind*. London: The Developing Company Press.

Lewin, Kurt. (1951). *Force field analysis*. New York: Harper and Row.

Mager, Robert F., and Peter Pipe (1984). *Analyzing Performance Problems or You Really Oughta Wanna*. Pitman Learning.

Manuele, Fred (2002). *Heinrich Revisited: Truisms or Myths*. National Safety Council.

Max, David (2009). *Whack-a-Mole: The Price We Pay for Expecting Perfection*. Eden Prairie: By Your Side Studios.

Miller, G. A. (1956) The magical number seven, plus or minus two: Some limits on our capacity for processing information, *Psychological Review*, 63[2]: 81–97.

MindManager Software, produced by Corel Corporation, www.mindmanager.com

Phillips, Gary (2008). *The Art of Safety*. Thunder Bay: OH&S Press.

Phillips, Gary. The Self-Correcting Organization Workshop. Northwest Training and Development, - See Self-Correcting Resources page following the Index

Robbins, Stever. *Newsletter*, www.steverrobbins.com

Slovic, Paul (2010). *The Feeling of Risk*. New York and Canada: Earthscan.

Smith-Chong, Jennifer and Dennis Chong (2017). *Do You Know How Another Knows To Be?* Oakville: C–Jade Publishing.

Smith-Chong, Jennifer and Dennis Chong (1991). *Don't Ask Why?* C–Jade Publications.

INDEX

SELF-CORRECTING RESOURCES

Quantity discounts

Quantity discounts on purchase of *The Self-Correcting Organization* are available to organizations, educational institutions and associations for re-selling, educational purposes, employee presentations, conferences, customer promotions, subscription incentives or fund-raisers.

Professional Speaking – Gary Phillips

Gary is available for corporate presentations, training, and conference events.

> "My gracious Gary...you should have read
> the comments by the audience.
> They were phenomenal!!! Best conference
> that they have had in years."
> Cathy Payne-Davis, Suncor

Please contact us directly.

Wallet cards of the "What's the Issue" questions are also available in volume discounts for distribution to employees.

Contact us at:
NW Training and Development
nwtd@tbaytel.net
(807) 622-6077
www.nwtd.ca or at www.selfcorrecting.ca

ABOUT THE AUTHOR

Gary Phillips has been a firefighter, Health and Safety Professional (CRSP), Human Resource Professional (CHRL), consultant, trainer, student (MA adult education) and a 3 chord guitar player. He alleges to have recovered from them all. Apparently unable to maintain a focus on any one of these areas he has chosen to develop integrated models that pull together patterns from across the spectrum of human performance.

His ongoing work in organizational and Leadership development, trainer and management training, personal and executive coaching, and writing, have somewhat limited his 3 chord performances to the relief of friends and family alike.

Gary is also the author of *The Art of Safety*.

A sought after trainer and speaker he has presented across North America and abroad from his home in Thunder Bay, Ontario Canada.